THE
INFINITE VIEW

THE INFINITE VIEW

A Guidebook for Life on Earth

ELLEN TADD

A TarcherPerigee Book

tarcherperigee

An imprint of Penguin Random House LLC
375 Hudson Street
New York, New York 10014

Most TarcherPerigee books are available at special quantity discounts for bulk purchase for sales promotions, premiums, fund-raising, and educational needs. Special books or book excerpts also can be created to fit specific needs. For details, write: SpecialMarkets@penguinrandomhouse.com.

ISBN 9780399175466

Printed in the United States of America
1   3   5   7   9   10   8   6   4   2

Book design by Elke Sigal

CONTENTS

CONTENTS

Do not be caught in the limited perspective of life, for it has continual turmoil and uncertainty. If you venture deeper, you will see that there is a growth plan in operation for all individuals. Go deep within the silence of your own being, and when you have heard, carry it through to completion with the full acceptance and knowledge of the infinite perspective of growth and evolution. Your world is rapidly changing. So begin now this listening, for it will be of greater need in the future.

— A Guide

Author's Note
The italicized passages at the beginning of each chapter are direct quotations from my guides.

CHAPTER ONE

The Journey to My Guides

We shall ascend the mountain together.
We shall climb to the highest peaks and there
the magnificent view of all of life shall be our reward.

I always say that my mother gave me birth and my mother gave me rebirth. On the first occasion she gave me physical life. On the second, when I was nineteen, she opened my mind to the world beyond the physical—an experience that led to a transformative understanding of why I'd often felt anxious and uncertain growing up, unable to plunge into life without a deeper comprehension of its meaning. That encounter set me on the path to meeting the spiritual guides and teachers who have since become the most powerful influences in my life, offering me tools and insights through which to navigate both the ordinary and extraordinary challenges of daily living.

Let me explain.

As a child, I had experiences that no one else around me seemed to share. At night, I saw faces in the dark, and although my father tried to reassure me that they were merely the work of a vivid imagination, I begged him to let me sleep with my light on. Sometimes I had out-of-body experiences: I'd be lying on my bed, when suddenly the room would start to spin, and "I" was on the ceiling looking down at "my" body still on the bed. *How can this be?* I wondered. *Am I the body on the bed, or am I on the ceiling? Who am I?*

Sometimes I saw light around people. I told my father, a physicist, "Daddy, I can see molecules!"—a word I'd learned from him. He replied that no one can see molecules with the naked eye, and to prove his point he brought me to an electron microscope laboratory at Yale University, where he was on sabbatical, to show me what molecules really looked like. As I watched the microscope screen I understood that he was right, of course. But if I wasn't seeing molecules, what was I seeing? Not knowing scared me.

Other times, I was overwhelmed by so many feelings and impressions that I couldn't even begin to sort them out, much less interpret them. In fifth grade, I remember missing an entire math lesson because I was so absorbed by the images and insights I was picking up about my teacher's personal life. I was also distracted by the fascinating nature of this ability.

I questioned my friends and other family members to see if they had similar experiences. They thought I was making up stories, so I learned to keep quiet about my unusual episodes. Although I spent a great deal of time feeling misunderstood and confused (spending time alone in nature was one of my few solaces), I always felt loved by my family. But as time passed I grew increasingly anxious.

This anxiety was rooted in some ways in a terrible shock that hit my family when I was very young. At the age of thirty-two, my mother woke one morning to discover that she was blind, the first sign of what would eventually be diagnosed as multiple sclerosis. The disease progressed rapidly, affecting both her mind and her body. If my mother was sick, I thought, perhaps I was, too.

Over the years, as I watched her deteriorate mentally and physically, I wanted to understand *why* my mother, who was a good person and loved us all so much, suffered so. I asked many such "why" questions, but no one provided me with satisfactory answers. Though I was raised without religion and felt agnostic, I took a tour of churches in our area when I was around ten or eleven, to see if religion could offer any resolution. I didn't find a source of information that felt personal or persuasive, nor did there seem to be much tolerance for my most pressing questions.

When I was seventeen, my mother died, paralyzed and unable to talk. The following year, I went to college, where I hoped to find a better understanding of life's meaning in books and classes on psychology and philosophy. I wanted to believe what I heard in lectures and seminars and embrace the concepts in books I was assigned, but I didn't feel certainty or confidence in the material presented. My life would have been easier if I had, but I didn't know if the ideas were actually true.

I frequently wrote in journals, continuing to ask myself questions and searching for peace of mind. After my first year in college, I decided to take a leave of absence and travel. Privately,

I resolved that during that year of exploration I would find my life's purpose. A friend told me about having had mystical experiences in Cuernavaca, Mexico, so I decided to go there. I was ready to be open to whatever came my way.

SPIRITUAL AWAKENING

Before arranging for my leave of absence, I visited one of my brothers, who lived and worked in New York City. At that time, he was dating a woman named Catherine, who called herself a trance medium—which I thought was very odd. Although I did have something of a mystical streak, and had wrestled with questions about the meaning and purpose of life, mediums and clairvoyants didn't really fit into my scheme of things. I'd certainly never met one in person.

A few moments after my brother introduced us, Catherine asked me, "Is there anyone who is dead that you'd like to speak with?"

Her blunt question startled me, but I managed to reply, "I don't know if I believe in life after death. But if I can, I'd like to speak with my mother."

Catherine didn't know about my mother, as she hadn't been dating my brother for very long; because my brother was rather reserved about emotional issues, he hadn't said much about our painful family situation. I didn't tell her, either, because at that point anything to do with my mother had been banished to a private, locked-up room of my psyche—one tinged with the misplaced guilt of a sensitive child with a very ill and suffering parent.

That evening, Catherine invited me into her apartment, just two floors below my brother's in the same building on Thompson Street. As she sat down to meditate, I waited and watched as her cats literally jumped off the walls and ran into the bathroom, apparently reacting to something I couldn't see. Many emotions and childhood memories swirled inside me as Catherine went into a trance. My mother had entered a nursing home when I was only eight years old, and as the years passed she became less and less a presence in my life; in many ways I hardly knew her. Then all of a sudden Catherine was lying down, in what looked to me like a paralyzed state, and to my surprise, I saw my mother's face superimposed over hers. The difference in their appearance was unmistakable. Catherine was blond and had a wide, round Slavic-looking face; my mother had a narrower face with high cheekbones and dark brown hair mixed with gray.

Then with great effort, my mother spoke to me. I had to bend over Catherine to hear, but it was my mother's voice, without a doubt.

"Do not mourn for me," she said, "for I chose what I endured." She then went on to say that no matter how things appear on the surface, "if you look deep enough, you will see there are always reasons and justice."

She told me she forgave me for all the things I'd done that were not quite right, because I'd only been a child—a statement that immediately released an enormous sense of guilt I'd unknowingly been carrying. She spoke to me about the process of reincarnation and told me that in previous lives she'd been selfish and arrogant. (Many years later, I had visions of my mother in a former life in ancient Rome, where she'd been an aristocrat with significant power, and had ignored the suffering of many people around her.) During her incarnation as my mother, she continued, she'd learned through her own suffering that we are all connected, and that if we ignore the struggles of others, we ignore our own. That was the justice to be found in the suffering she endured in her most recent life: She'd acquired the capacity to experience and express genuine compassion.

For me, her statement, *If you look deep enough, there are always reasons and justice,* was a revelation. It meant that life had order; it wasn't just chaos and cruelty, as it had often appeared to me. Faced so immediately and intimately with reincarnation—and the opportunity for learning that comes with it—I found that life all at once began to make sense. There were reasons why things transpired as they did. I began to feel more pleasure in being alive.

Communicating with my mother on a spiritual plane also brought into sharp and dramatic focus the sensitivity I'd experienced since childhood. After that session, Catherine went upstairs to spend the night with my brother, while I stayed in her apartment. But I realized I wasn't alone: Entities and spirits could be all around me, and know my thoughts. For the first time, I grasped that no aspect of my life was completely private. Initially that awareness felt frightening and embarrassing, though now it feels comforting to be completely seen and never feel alone.

Unable to sleep that night, I read a book on palmistry I found on Catherine's bookshelf. The next day, I was amazed to discover that when I looked at people's palms, I could see visions of their soul's journey—an ability, I later learned, known as "hand scrying." On the bus back to college, I sat next to a woman who was obviously troubled. I plunged ahead. "Let me look at your hand," I asked her. She agreed, and I saw visions that enabled me to tell her about her life.

I continued to have more such clairvoyant experiences, which further opened me to phenomena I hadn't previously been conscious of or that once had frightened me. As I recalled my childhood episodes, I was able to look at them from the new perspective that my mother had brought to me.

I was certainly a spiritual novice at that point, beginning to be aware of my abilities, yet untrained in how to integrate them into my life. Not long after my first experience with Catherine (she and my brother had broken up by then but we were still friends), we visited an artist who had a collection of sculptures in his large and luxurious apartment. As the afternoon wore on the three of us found ourselves having a wide-ranging and amiable conversation. Suddenly, though, I found myself able to feel the unhappiness of this man who appeared to be surrounded by ease and privilege. Despite his talent, success, wealth, and apparent comfort he seemed lonely, embittered, and lost. Thinking it might help him, I began to talk about the experiences I'd had with my mother. I mentioned how much grief and guilt I'd suffered during her illness and death, and how that burden had lifted. I ventured further, telling him what I had begun to see and understand, and what I saw about his life.

To my surprise, he wasn't at all interested to hear what I had to say; in fact, he was quite hostile. "Who do you think you are, the Chosen One?" he asked. "You've been put on earth to tell people what their problems are, and what gives you the right to do that?"

I turned to Catherine, hoping for rescue, but she was as confused as I, and eventually we made as graceful an exit as possible. I went home that evening troubled. Did I think I was special, "chosen," put on earth to impart truths that others would rather not acknowledge? The idea seemed distasteful, arrogant. It hadn't been my intention to show off my specialness, but instead to offer something that could be useful. Clearly, I didn't know how.

SURPRISING ENCOUNTERS

Not long afterward, I went to Cuernavaca as I'd originally planned and attended a school started by Ivan Illich, a former Roman Catholic priest who promoted the idea that education isn't confined solely to formal classrooms and structured class periods; rather, life itself is a school. I stayed in an old mansion on a beautiful estate, which I shared with an interesting group of people from around the world who were drawn to Illich's idea of "de-schooling" society.

While in Cuernavaca, I spent many afternoons at an English-language bookstore. At that time, I gravitated toward books that discussed spiritual topics, most of which advocated meditation, and after asking around a bit, I located a place that taught yoga and meditation. I attended only one class, but it was a fascinating and unusual experience, because the teacher and all the students in the class spoke Spanish, a language I didn't know. Very carefully, I observed everyone and followed along. The first part of the class was devoted to practicing yoga postures; then the men headed into the men's locker room and the women into the women's locker room to take showers. I shadowed a friendly older woman who spoke some broken English, and while we were getting dressed she explained that we must be clean and fresh before meditation.

After we all returned to the large open space, everyone sat in lotus position and closed their eyes to meditate. The teacher gave what I assumed was some formal instruction, which I couldn't understand. I relied on my memory of what I had read about meditation—simply that meditation is an inner stillness, a holding one's thoughts at bay, so that was what I did. I discovered that I was a natural meditator. I was able to keep my mind still for long periods without much effort, just as I had as a child, when, for instance, I'd stare out a window with my mind free of thoughts. After that one afternoon, I started to sit in stillness as a regular practice.

One day at the English-language bookstore, I met an American man, an actor who was interested in making a film based on a book called *A World Beyond*, by a then-famous medium named Ruth Montgomery. Montgomery was living in Cuernavaca at the time, and after this man explained who he was and showed me some newspaper clippings to verify that he had been on Broadway, he asked if I knew her. I didn't, but without thinking, I told him that as a child I'd had experiences leaving my body, and if we could find a quiet place to meditate, I thought I could do so again and locate her. I have no idea what possessed me to tell him that; I suppose I felt cocky and confident.

Perhaps because he was interested in meditation and spiritual phenomena, he didn't appear startled, and we seemed to feel swept up in something larger than both of us. This unusual exchange just felt right. I brought him to the garden of the estate where I was staying and together we meditated on a bench, surrounded by lush vegetation and flowers. The sensation of leaving my body was familiar to me: first a feeling of expansion, then more expansion, and then a kind of swirling out of my dense physical body, leaving me only in my lighter etheric form.

Gradually I noticed that I was floating close to the ceiling in a room I didn't recognize, looking down at a woman in bed wearing a bed jacket and nestled against her pillows, reading a book. (Years later I saw a photograph of Montgomery and I'm convinced she was the woman I saw.) A man in a body that appeared less solid than the woman's hovered near me. I had learned that Ruth Montgomery's book was based partly on her communications with her friend and mentor Arthur Ford, who served as a spirit guide to her after his death. I thought this floating man might be Ford, though I was never able to confirm that. When I approached him, full of curiosity, he surprised me by reprimanding me very sternly, saying, "You don't know what you're doing; you're playing with fire." I was so startled, I abruptly found myself back in my body, sitting on the bench in the garden.

We ended our experiment, and the actor eventually found Ruth Montgomery through more conventional means. But I got the message: Just because I had an ability didn't mean I knew how to use it. My education would need to be meticulous, rigorous, and thorough. It was not to be separate, either, from my life lessons, but woven into everyday living.

MEETING MY GUIDES

Not long after these events, I met a man, fell in love, got married, and settled down to make a home in a rural area of Massachusetts. One night in the depths of a New England winter, I was nursing a bad case of the flu; my husband was sleeping on the couch to let me get some rest. At three in the morning I woke to see a small face with Asian features, floating in the air above me. His skin appeared as moving, scintillating light, and he radiated purity, unconditional love, and a compassion I'd never experienced before. I knew this being was completely trustworthy and wanted only the best for me. No words or specific messages were expressed, and I have no idea how much time passed during this encounter, but after a while he vanished, leaving me feeling deeply loved, secure, and protected.

After this first encounter with my Asian guide, as I started calling him, he and other spiritual entities began coming to me periodically while I was meditating or performing daily activities, appearing in forms I could both see and hear. At first, when they offered insights, I'd sit down with a pen and a pad of paper and write down exactly what they said as they spoke. Later, they began transmitting most of their instructions and wisdom either via thought or through visions that appeared in my mind's eye—and often a combination of both. The times when I would hear an audible voice or see external visions were the most penetrating and personally moving forms of contact. At one point, I asked if they would identify themselves by name. I was told, "In your world people are enamored with identity, so we wish to remain anonymous, so that our messages will stand on their own."

I'm well aware that a conventionally trained mental health professional would suggest a very different explanation for all of this. The thinking would probably run along the lines that following the death of my mother and at an age when many young people feel vulnerable and on the edge of instability, I was suffering psychotic episodes. To this I can only respond that after these types of experiences I became emotionally stronger. I began to locate my own moral and intellectual compass and learn to follow it. I felt I'd entered the school of life, receiving the education I'd long been seeking, from individuals who really did comprehend life's meaning and purpose. I was learning how to live as a sensitive in an insensitive world.

It was a tremendous relief to discover that the receptiveness I'd experienced since childhood could be trained and transformed from a social liability into a precise skill for understanding human complexity. Up until that point, if I walked into a room where someone had a stomachache or a headache, I often came down with one as well. I was an emotional sponge, often overwhelmed by other people's feelings; as I result, I tended to shut down and withdraw from relationships, even though I was popular and sought out by my peers. Because my receptivity had made the world seem difficult to navigate, the first lessons my guides offered me involved learning how to become a positive influence rather than being negatively affected by my environment.

Other initial teachings were philosophical in nature, such as an explanation of the difference between acceptance and complacency. I was taught that many people are uncomfortable with the notion of acceptance, equating it with a kind of laziness or avoidance of experiences or ideas that appear too challenging or confusing. My guides, however, stress that acceptance is simply the acknowledgment of what is because it is. It's a spiritual principle that brings us peace: When we stop fighting or avoiding, turbulent emotions cease, and in the calm that follows, insights spontaneously emerge and appropriate responses become more apparent.

DEEPER EDUCATION

The process of developing relationships with my etheric guides and teachers has continued over many years. Some of them have offered direction in managing the tasks and concerns of daily life, while others have focused more specifically on philosophy, tools, and techniques to help me become an effective teacher. Of course, some have provided both aspects of my education.

One particularly significant event occurred when I was meditating with friends in my living room. I had a vision, off to my right, of a Native American man coming toward me. As I watched him move closer, I suddenly—and for the first time— felt my consciousness pushed aside, over to the left, while the man began to use my body to speak. He spoke eloquently about the power of nature as a spiritual teacher. I wasn't able to hear all his words, but when I returned to my body my friends were in awe. They'd heard a voice that was not mine coming from me, and it was clear that my body had been inhabited by a spirit guide. His elevated consciousness remained with me for a time, expanding my perceptions beyond my normal awareness. From this state, it felt marvelous to simply be a part of the miracle of life.

For a while after this encounter, I became a trance medium. I still have this gift, but I began to feel too much like a telephone, mechanically transmitting information made available through me. I longed to participate more fully in receiving the knowledge being conveyed. I didn't want people to see me as an authority figure, either, because I knew I was a student, learning and striving to learn. I asked my guides and teachers from the spiritual realm to work with me more regularly through clairvoyance and clairaudience, so I could continue to be the student I knew I was and serve as a teacher only when it was appropriate.

An important time during this period of developing communication with my guides and spiritual teachers was when my two children were young. Often a guide would offer instruction while I was engaged with my children or involved in some domestic activity, such as making dinner or folding laundry, which greatly enhanced my pleasure in everyday chores. Sometimes the communications were personal and extremely pragmatic. One day, for instance, while I was folding T-shirts and jeans, a guide told me to be patient with my four-year-old son's outbursts, explaining that my son saw himself as an adult and resented being treated like a child. He said that my son's frustration would dissipate after he learned to read and to ride a bicycle, because he'd no longer feel as though he were held captive in a small body. That, indeed, is what happened.

In the early days of my education, I sometimes became

discouraged when I made mistakes—such as falling into negative attitudes or being careless in my choice of words or actions—that my guides had corrected over and over again, for they were intent on teaching me to actualize my spiritual nature in my daily life. I'd also grow discouraged by the actions of others. Even today I sometimes feel disheartened. But my guides never become discouraged. They never waver in their certainty that everyone will eventually succeed in actualizing their spiritual potential. Who wouldn't want to be with such loving, supportive individuals?

My connection and communication with my guides has been a deep and powerful schooling at every level: intellectual, moral, emotional, and practical. They've helped me through some tremendously challenging periods. On various occasions they've intervened in ways that literally saved my life and the lives of my children. They've trained me for a successful career as a teacher and counselor, prodded me along an arduous path to true love, and taught me what I believe to be keys to living a fulfilling life. Their wisdom, pragmatism, and unswerving belief in the essential goodness of every person have inspired me to integrate their teachings into every aspect of my life.

A CONTINUING EVOLUTION

Along the journey, my guides led me to write this book.

Their teachings are, of course, the source of the concepts and practices described in the following pages. The way I learned to present these teachings can be traced back to a period some thirty years ago, when they asked me to teach a series of classes presenting what I'd learned from them to other people. I'd never seen myself as a teacher, never seen myself in front of a class. Still, I agreed to their request, without really knowing what I was getting into or having any time to prepare. At that point in my life, I was in the middle of a divorce, raising two small children, and building my private practice as a clairvoyant counselor, all while navigating the large and small details involved in having a new house built.

This is how the classes came to be: One evening a week, I'd climb into my Subaru station wagon, joined by a spirit guide, who had been a philosopher and a wordsmith in his last incarnation, in nineteenth-century England. During the twenty-five-minute drive from my home to Amherst he discussed the topic I'd present that night and the exercises I'd teach, all the while infusing me with confidence and clarity. Although I had no time to write anything down, I was able to conduct twenty-three classes, and when the entire series was completed I saw a clear link between each class and an organization that extended from the first to the last. My guide had orchestrated the entire series for me.

This book represents a synthesis of the lessons my guides have offered me, which I pass along in classes and workshops I continue to teach. My hope in presenting this material more widely is to demystify the mystical, expand the cultural view of who we are and what life is about, and demonstrate that direct spiritual experiences are available to everyone. As a student and a teacher, I see my role as that of a proponent of an infinite spiritual perspective and of the means of integrating that perspective into daily living.

The central focus of each chapter is explored in a variety of ways, since the concepts are multifaceted and aspects of each often overlap. This approach reproduces an essential characteristic of my guides' process of teaching, for they often return to a subject to help me expand my understanding of it.

For example, sometimes my guides will pull me aside and say, "Now you are going to learn about compassion."

"I've already done that," I might reply.

"Yes," they'll answer, "but we're going deeper now." In the same way, some concepts introduced in early chapters will be explored more deeply in later ones.

I tell many stories in these pages—about myself, about people I know, and about experiences in the classes I've taught. In part, these stories serve to illustrate how the tools and principles have worked for me and for others who have chosen to integrate them into their lives, and how they can work for you.

But they also serve a larger function. My father was a scientist, a man trained to seek empirical evidence to support his ideas and the ideas of his colleagues and contemporaries. Growing up in a household where that method was emphasized has shaped my own approach. I understand very well that our culture gives little credence to many of the subjects I discuss here, such as the existence and influence of past lives, and the idea that each of us is on a path of evolution that extends through many lifetimes toward a future of enlightenment. I myself would have doubts were it not for the confirmation that has come from my own experience and the experiences of people I trust, and from the fact that thousands of students in my classes have trained themselves to become sensitive to what I might call the "reality of Spirit."

To skeptics I would say: Try the practices I present. See what happens. Let your own life be your testing ground.

I would also add that early in my own spiritual education, I asked my guides the questions that had been put to me by the man who had been so angered by my first, halting attempt to describe my experiences: Who am I? Have I been "chosen"? And if so, why—and for what?

The answer I received from my guides: Yes, I was chosen. In fact, we are all chosen.

Individually and collectively, we're all engaged in a process of transformation. For many of us, the changes that occur within and around us seem beyond our control, leaving us with a feeling of helplessness, anxiety, and confusion. But that apparent powerlessness is an illusion, an error of thought and perception that can be corrected through opening ourselves to the authentic core of wisdom, creativity, and compassion with which we are all inherently gifted.

The tools and practices presented in this book are not meant only for the "spiritual few." They are available to every living being. My guides have given me concepts and practices that I continue to explore and integrate into my life, the full implications of which I've tested for myself. However, we each have free will and choice, and each of us must live our own lives. Guides don't set out instructions or "recipes" to be followed to the letter. Instead, they tell us where and how to look. We must do the looking and decide what we see.

CHAPTER TWO

Who Are We and Why Are We Here?

I see you all as an interconnected web
of individuals forming Oneness.

The encounter with my mother that night in Catherine's apartment marked a profound spiritual awakening, and I began to experience the effects immediately. When I stepped out onto Thompson Street the next morning, the colors of the world had intensified, and though I'd been flooded with many different emotions, I felt immensely lighter. I walked for a long time through the crowded streets of Manhattan, even though I'd grown up in a small town and wasn't used to being surrounded by so many people at once. As I made my way through the crowds, I became aware that my view of the world had been turned on its head. I'd spent so much of my life doubting ministers, questioning teachers, rejecting textbooks, and even setting aside my own unusual experiences, but the core of what had occurred was incontestable. I began to sense and feel the wheels of a vast justice turning in the universe, a movement much larger than anything I could have conceived; it was almost beyond comprehension.

While I wandered through the busy streets teeming with individuals, I was filled with the certainty that everyone was a spiritual being in human form. I found myself deeply moved on so many levels, and amazed that I'd never before seen what now seemed so obvious. I realized, too, that most people didn't remember who they were or why they were here, and that somehow part of my life's purpose was to help people to remember—though at that point I didn't quite know how to go about it.

Eight years later, the belief that we are all spiritual beings manifesting temporarily on earth was definitively confirmed for me when I clairvoyantly watched my son incarnate. At the beginning of my labor, I had a vivid external vision of three men in etheric form standing at the foot of my bed: a tall, thin young man dressed in pants and a jacket standing between two older men dressed in robes. All three were surrounded by shimmering golden light. Somehow I knew that the young man was my unborn son. In thought, I heard him say, "I've just come to see if you are all right." I told him I was, and I remember thinking, "Oh good, I'm going to have a considerate son and a short labor." Subsequently, the three of them disappeared.

In fact, my interpretation was wrong in one respect: I had a very long labor and ended up going to the hospital twice.

The first time I stayed for a few hours before I was sent home to rest for half a day. On the way to the hospital for the second time, my son again appeared in etheric form. He was alone this time, and his etheric body looked small enough to stand up fully in the car. Suddenly, his form began to dissolve, from the top of his head and simultaneously from the bottom of his feet, until all that remained was a beam of white light, which entered the physical form of the child I was carrying. Two hours later my son was born. It became clear to me that though I was providing a vehicle, the essence of my son's being existed before the creation of his body. He was an individual on his own life's path.

As I watched the doctor, nurses, and my husband welcome our son into the world, I was filled with compassion for all people, for we have all traversed the spiritual realm to come to the earth. It takes great courage to be born, to move from an unrestricted realm into a limited body. As infants, we're completely dependent on others to care for us. We need to learn how to feed ourselves, walk independently, communicate through language, and so much more. The process of developing into adults is a long and humbling experience for all of us, and as we progress through childhood into adulthood we're exposed to a variety of confusing and contradictory cultural messages, many of which obscure the true nature of our identity and purpose.

SPIRIT IS OUR ESSENCE

The educational system in many modern cultures encourages us to believe that individual identity is shaped mainly by genetics and environmental influences—nature and nurture. However, I've learned from my guides and confirmed through my own experiences that identity is actually made up of three aspects: the Spirit, the soul, and the personality. The core of our being is Spirit, the essence of life, the conscious and communicative force present in all things, even those we ordinarily perceive as inanimate. This aspect of our being is our enlightened self: always compassionate, always loving, always wise, and always creative. It is the only constant, continuing from one life to the next and one dimension to the next. It is the infinite, interconnected life force, the Oneness that pervades everything yet simultaneously manifests as the essence of every individual being, which my guides refer to as the "Spirit within."

The Spirit within is the particular essence of an individual. Like snowflakes, no two individual expressions of Spirit are identical. In my classes, I often use the analogy of light and color to help people understand the relationship between the Oneness and the Spirit within. White light is made up of all the colors of the visible spectrum, which appear separately when dispersed through a prism. The Oneness that infuses and empowers all things can be thought of as white light. When expressed as an individual Spirit, a person's spiritual essence corresponds to a tint or shade of a particular color in this infinite spectrum.

My guides consistently emphasize the importance of learning to connect both with the Oneness and with our own inner Spirit. Consciously connecting with the Oneness is a remarkable experience, filled with ecstasy, bliss, and a profound sense of awe in the power and order of the universe. Although my guides had told me often during the early years of their lessons that everything is conscious, communicating, and interconnected, I didn't truly grasp what that meant until one weekend when I was teaching a workshop in the Catskill Mountains. The workshop had gone very well; contented, joyful feelings filled the conference room, and our group meditations were deep and satisfying. When we broke for lunch, I stepped outside the conference center into a beautiful October day and was startled to see glowing light around every rock and leaf. All around me I heard a choral symphony. Everything in nature was singing, "I am alive! I am alive!"

Eventually I found my way to the cafeteria building and went to the ladies' room. When I looked at myself in the mirror, I saw, more deeply than I ever had, that I was Spirit. Light surrounded me in the mirror, and as I studied my reflection I knew I was much more than a brain and a body. In that moment I felt completely that I was part of the Oneness, and the immensity of that sensation began to penetrate my consciousness in a way that entirely transcended intellectual comprehension.

Immersed in the experience of Oneness, I was aware, too, of simply being Ellen. That was another revelation: I could feel the power and purity of flowing in an infinite interconnected whole and yet simultaneously recognize myself as just one small individual. Suddenly, it felt so easy to love myself. I realized that once we're truly able to perceive ourselves as Spirit, we can see that we're more than our mistakes or our accomplishments. At this core level we are all magnificent.

Spirit encompasses a full range of qualities I've been taught to refer to as spiritual principles—such as love, wisdom, devotion, order, creativity, and curiosity. According to my guides, spiritual principles are always applicable and always appropriate. We can't have too much balance, or too much clarity, or too much compassion.

At the same time, the Spirit within each of us manifests a distinctive emphasis, which I often think of as our particular instrument in the orchestra of life. This emphasis may be kindness or creativity; it may be wisdom or love. It can sometimes be quite nuanced, like variations of ice cream flavors. I often use this analogy: Some people are pure vanilla, while others are vanilla with chocolate or strawberry swirls. The potential combinations are limitless.

For example, I work with a variety of people whose emphasis is creativity, but the way their creativity is expressed in terms of interests and talents reflects subtle differences. While one person's emphasis may incline toward sound and be expressed as a talent for playing or composing music, another may be drawn to visual harmony, expressed as a talent for interior design. Sometimes I'll work with someone whose individual spiritual expression of creativity is very flexible, so the style of expression doesn't seem to matter.

It's entirely possible for people to discover their own particular spiritual emphasis, though it will likely require practicing some of the tools in this book. I'd been meditating and listening to my guides for many years before I learned that my individual emphasis is gentle wisdom, and that I need to find my strength through my gentleness. This understanding resulted from my efforts to parent my daughter when she was young. Her spiritual nature is more forceful than mine, and in trying to parent her well, at times I attempted to meet her strength head-on, which meant being quite tough. When my guide pointed out that my emphasis is gentle wisdom, I was told I should find my power in my gentleness. That doesn't mean that I can be pushed around or that I should allow myself to be pushed around; like bamboo, I can be delicate yet still strong.

THE SOUL: THE CONTAINER OF THE SPIRIT

The second aspect of our identity is the soul, the container of our Spirit, through which our distinct nature retains its uniqueness within the Oneness. When our physical body dies, our inner Spirit and soul leave together, and we maintain individuality even after death. In describing the relationship between the Spirit and the soul, I often use the analogy of an appliance, such as a toaster oven. Just as electricity provides the power to enable a toaster oven to function, so Spirit activates and animates the soul. The analogy isn't perfect, of course. The soul is very complicated and—unlike toaster ovens— always evolving.

The soul holds the records of all of our past-life patterns, experiences, fears, and traumas, as well as the talents and skills we've accumulated through all the lives we've lived. The accumulation of past-life experiences is different for each of us, of course, just as our experiences during our present lives differ from those of other people. When we incarnate, we're guided toward parents and circumstances that activate and arouse our soul's patterns—both our strengths and our weaknesses—in order to move us toward learning the lessons we need so that we can heal past imbalances residing in the soul and fully actualize our spiritual nature.

I was able to directly observe past-life patterns inscribed in the soul almost immediately after my mother communicated with me from the spiritual realm. As I described earlier, hand scrying offered me my first access to the soul and its record of past lives. As I gazed into people's palms, I saw visions—like a movie in my mind's eye—of each person as male in some lives and female in others. They wore clothing of bygone eras, and interacted in environments that were clearly not the present. The images of the events of their past lives unfolded in my mind's eye with great detail and emotion.

During the first few years of my work as a clairvoyant counselor, I simply relayed the past-life stories I received. For my clients, these sessions were full of revelations, synchronicity, and fascinating material, but I sensed I had more to learn. People came to me because they wanted to better understand and deal with the problems facing them, to receive help that was afforded in no other quarter of life—and I wanted to contribute.

One day, while tracing a client's evolution through her lifetimes, I discerned a serene, fulfilled life in which she'd experienced none of the chronic, repetitive patterns of burdened over-responsibility she faced in many lives, including her present one. It was a pleasure to tune in to her healthy, balanced incarnation. But what, I wondered, had happened? How had she—and, as I soon began to perceive, others—left this state? What had shifted to produce lifetimes of difficulty?

I began to look more carefully for these "fulfilled" lives as sources of information. Then I sought out incarnations in which a challenging situation arose and examined how the challenge was met. My aim was to ascertain how these lives were linked. How did fulfillment devolve into frustrated desires? Happiness turn to tragedy? How were talents and gifts rewarded in some lifetimes, only to be blocked and thwarted in later ones? Why did so many feel helpless to create change in their lives, almost as though they were spellbound by mysterious forces?

FIRST ERROR AND THE BEGINNING OF THE "KARMIC SNOWBALL"

As I investigated the soul more deeply, mainly through performing past-life readings for clients, I'd often see a lot of repetition. Certain soul patterns began to look to me like a kind of groove. Lifetime after lifetime, people would become caught in that groove, repeating the same mistakes and suffering the same consequences. Gradually, I was able to identify a very deep pattern, which I call "first error": a misconception or misperception that is not in harmony with our spiritual essence, creating an imbalance that disrupts our alignment with our spiritual consciousness.

In some respects, this disruption resembles the Christian concept of original sin. I've learned through working with large numbers of people, however, that first error is not inherited; nor is it the same for everyone. Just as everyone's spiritual essence is a little different, so is everyone's first error. We each have our own particular brand of fear, our own particular imbalance.

According to my guides, in the beginning of our incarnation process, we were able to actualize our spiritual nature consistently. Over successive incarnations, most of us succumb to a first error misconception or misperception. Our ability to actualize becomes imbalanced or constrained, triggering a kind of "karmic snowball." Behaviors and attitudes arising out of that original imbalance, and the consequences of repeating them, create a self-defeating life pattern.

After years of tracing people's reincarnation process back to their earliest error, I found two fundamental categories of imbalance: an inner first error and an outer first error. An inner first error stems from a misperception about oneself. An outer first error stems from faulty perceptions of others.

One example of an inner first error to which I can point involved a client of mine who had been motivated by her loving nature to come to the earth to help alleviate human suffering. In her past, she incarnated in an enlightened state as a healer and helper, providing insight and comfort to many, but some people resisted her help and others were critical of her efforts. Internalizing this rejection, she began to doubt her capacity as a healer and concluded that she must not be good enough. Her fear of being inadequate was her first error. To counter this fear, she set out to deflect it by proving her worth to others. She projected herself as superior, acting as though she knew everything and responding to everyone's needs and problems, even when it wasn't appropriate. The attempt to solve every problem snowballed into deeper feelings of insufficiency, setting the stage for a karmic pattern of inadequacy and overcompensation.

As an example of an outer first error, I recall a man who

first incarnated in a leadership role. His Spirit of powerful depth gave him great wisdom. As a leader he was motivated to create a harmonious, thriving culture, but the situation surrounding him did not go well, spiraling out of his control into war. Nonetheless, though he believed in his own competence, he doubted the capacity of others to implement his wise counsel, triggering a first error of feeling overly responsible, even for situations over which he had no influence. After this initial incarnation, he returned many times as a monk or scholar, so he could focus inwardly on his own Spirit and avoid external conditions he couldn't control. To heal this imbalance, he needed to allow himself to fully be involved with the world, offering his spiritual contribution of wisdom and power to the best of his ability, while learning that he could influence, but not control, outcomes.

Recognizing the impact of past-life experiences recorded in the soul can help us understand our fears, choices, and experiences in our current life more clearly, as well as our relationships with and reactions to other people. Say, for example, you're involved in a certain relationship—maybe with a friend or a lover—and you can't quite figure out why you're drawn together. It's possible that you're here to support each other because of a harmonious pattern of relationship in previous lives. Maybe you need to learn lessons that you didn't learn earlier, such as the ability to say no when you're being abused in some way. Perhaps the relationship is meant to offer you the opportunity to move past the fear of rejection. There are any number of reasons why we're drawn to certain relationships, and in my experience they're always connected to past-life circumstances.

Understanding the role of soul lessons can also give us access to deeper matters of purpose. I once worked with a woman who had previously incarnated many times as a man, and in this life she became a lawyer. At the time I worked with her, the legal profession was a male-dominated field. While she didn't feel out of place, understanding the influence of her past lives increased her passion for her career as an attorney, because she came to appreciate that part of her purpose was to help expand professional roles for women.

PERSONALITY: OUR PERSONA IN THE WORLD

The third aspect of identity is personality: the characteristic patterns of thought, feeling, and behavior that mark each person as unique. A variety of factors affect the development of personality, including genetics, social and environmental conditioning, and specific events and experiences that occur at different stages in our lives. Based on my own work and the insights I've received from my guides, past-life experiences and the individual expression of our spiritual essence also play important roles.

For instance, my brother was a musician in a number of past lives. When we took music lessons together as children, he played easily while I could only kind of pluck along. At the time, I thought the difference between our abilities had something to do with me; I now know that it had more to do with him. Over many lifetimes, we all work hard at developing certain skills that eventually manifest as "gifts" or talents. My brother had honed his musical skills in previous lives, so music, composing, and performing came easily to him in the life we shared as siblings. In my own case, I focused on developing clairvoyance in prior incarnations and haven't had to work at it in this life; it's an aptitude that carried over.

CULTURAL IMPEDIMENTS

Unfortunately, many people aren't aware of these deep aspects of their own and others' identities. My guides explain this dilemma by saying, "What you focus on is what you see." This is a simple-sounding yet profound maxim, which we can easily test for ourselves. If we deliberately look for everything of a particular color in a room—red, for example—all the red objects shift to the foreground of our awareness.

The same principle applies to Spirit and our soul's patterns. If we focus on them, we begin to see them. However, even though Spirit is conscious and communicative—and our past lives influence our present-life attractions, aspirations, and fears—we haven't been taught to look for these aspects of ourselves and others. In fact, it's fair to say that most of us have been conditioned *not* to look for them. As children, we were taught to focus on identifying and naming objects, and to make distinctions based more or less superficially on appearance.

Many cultures also emphasize competition as a way of measuring human worth and achievement. In Western societies in particular, the race to win has encouraged a "zoomer" mentality that encourages us to identify a goal and figure out the fastest way to get there. One of my clients was a zoomer who focused all her energy on building her career and making a lot of money, which she succeeded in doing. But then her health declined, her relationship with her child deteriorated, and she began to feel a lot of grief about the loss of balance and integration in her life as a consequence of following society's prescription for success. How many people push themselves to get something they think they want, only to discover that they don't really want it?

Zooming also tempts us to ignore the value of the experiences we might accumulate as we move toward a goal. In my family we have a joke: "So you want to be a rock star, but you don't want to learn the chords." From the outset of our work together, my guides advised against taking shortcuts. "A shortcut," they said, "will negate your learning and your purpose."

SPIRIT HEALS THE SOUL

Two fundamental challenges make it difficult for us to actualize our spiritual nature: unresolved traumas and fears from previous lives that are rooted in our first error, and cultural conditioning that doesn't support the actualization of our enlightened self. According to my guides, the more challenging of the two is the barrage of cultural messages we receive—some tacit, others blatant—that are contrary to the wisdom of spiritual principles.

For example, I was recently told about a five-year-old girl who was having difficulty focusing in her kindergarten class. Her teacher asked the principal to have the girl tested for attention deficit hyperactivity disorder (ADHD), suggesting she be put on medication. Unfortunately, this is not an unusual scenario. We live in a society in which it's common to conclude that fidgety or rowdy children have ADHD—a syndrome—rather than seeking a more holistic approach, incorporating adjustments to diet, opportunities for exercise, and activities that inspire and encourage focus.

I compare this story to that of one of my brothers, who was rambunctious as a child but channeled his energy into becoming a serious long-distance runner; as an adult, he is a volunteer high school and college track coach. If he'd been a youngster today a teacher might have suggested that he be medicated. It's troubling to hear about the number of children who are "treated" with medication. If parents and teachers were informed by a spiritually attuned perspective, might they be more motivated to pursue a deeper investigation into what is most beneficial for each child to thrive?

If our cultural norms embraced and encouraged our spiritual nature, we would gradually unravel the negative patterns in our souls. As my guides say, "The Spirit heals the soul." In other words, when we feel, express, and manifest the spiritual qualities in our essence, we heal the fears and traumas from our previous incarnations that radically affect the quality of our current life. But if our conditioning confuses us with an onslaught of faulty attitudes and flawed demonstrations of how life should be lived, then the process of healing the soul becomes much more difficult—and along the way we may deepen our misperceptions and acquire other wounds.

Nevertheless, it is possible to break the hold of such unsupportive conditioning. The first step is to recognize it for what it is, to remember that we are more than our genetics and products of our environment. We are spiritual beings incarnated into situations that challenge us to grow beyond our confusion, mistakes, and misperceptions toward a state of consciousness in which we're able to access the magnificent qualities of our spiritual nature.

When I began to directly experience the spiritual dimension of my own being and of life around me, and embrace the concept that there were reasons why things transpired as they did, the turmoil I'd experienced previously began to shift into greater acceptance and deeper curiosity. I'm certainly not a master of the spiritual perspective, but in dealing with various experiences, I began to ask myself or my guides, "What does this mean? What is my lesson in this situation? What am I to learn?" I worked to step out of feeling torn by good-or-bad, right-or-wrong thinking, in order to cultivate a more universal perspective. I began to grasp and experience that I was here to learn, to contribute, and to enjoy the gift of the physical senses. Waking up in the morning with a feeling of purpose had the tremendous capacity to carry me through the day, even during periods of adversity.

SHIFTING FOCUS

One way to begin working through limiting conditioning and start to experience spiritual essence and the complexity of the soul is to change our focus. When we concentrate on looking beneath the surface to perceive the Spirit of an individual, the Spirit moves to the foreground—just like when we focus on a particular color—and we start to recognize it and feel connected to the essential goodness and beauty in everyone, no matter how people may appear.

The first time I was guided to practice this lesson, I was driving through an old Massachusetts mill town not far from where I was living. At a stoplight, a guide gently whispered to me to look deeply into people walking down the street. "Look past the appearance of these people," he said. "Bore with your mind into them, past their complexity into the simplicity of their essence." To help me focus, he told me to affirm, "I am Spirit and you are Spirit," which I steadily repeated to myself in my mind.

It might seem strange that I was told to practice seeing Spirit in people while driving. I think one reason was to teach me to perceive Spirit quickly, so the perception would be as quick and natural as noticing someone had brown hair—an experience I could integrate into a busy life of raising children and running errands. My guides had explained that I needed to shift my focus quickly, like loosing an arrow, or else I'd get bogged down by the complex impressions I received about an individual's past experiences and personality. They advised me to dodge and ignore the surface appearances and aim my consciousness at the spiritual essence alone.

I was often amazed at the beauty of the Spirit, the deepest self, of each person I perceived as I drove by them in my car. Outwardly, many of the people I focused on appeared unhappy, negative, or disheveled, but their Spirits were always beautiful. I often welled up with feelings of love.

ATTUNEMENT

My guides say we experience true fulfillment when we manifest our spiritual nature, when we bring forth the qualities of our Spirit in daily living. This is a vital point, because we've been trained and have adapted to the idea that happiness comes from getting what we want, whether it's a fancy new coat or world peace; if our desires aren't met, we're justified in feeling sad, angry, or hurt. When we change the definition of happiness to my guides' description of true fulfillment, then we cease being victims of our circumstances.

Life is over and under and up and down. No matter how hard we try, we can't hammer it flat; we can't control what goes on around us or make others behave in the way we want. If, instead, we put our focus on actualizing our spiritual nature and bringing our best self to a situation, we can develop a resilient, confident inner life and become strong, constructive influences in the world.

We all actualize spiritual principles at various moments in our lives, sometimes spontaneously and sometimes with more directed intention. For example, years ago a Buddhist neighbor told me a story about a married man who had decided to become a monk; he left his wife and children to devote all his time to meditation. Then his wife became ill and he was called upon to return to take care of her and their children. He realized that if he wanted to continue his Buddhist meditation practices, he'd have to integrate them into his daily efforts to care for his family, so he developed different techniques of spiritual practice that became part of his everyday routines. I've since heard many variations of this sort of occurrence, but the main point is always the same: The world is always with us. The question is, how do we want to live in the world?

Each of us is like a river finding its way to the sea, engaged in a journey back to Oneness—consciousness in individual form. Whether we want to make this voyage or not, life will push us toward engaging in a process of healing our soul and learning to sustain the experience and the expression of spiritual principles. The will of our Spirit supersedes our personality's desires and misperceptions. No matter what mistakes I made, no matter how out-of-bounds my behavior was, my guides were very clear up front that my essential nature is Spirit and therefore I am good. That will never change. From that foundation, they stepped forward to try to help me to align my conscious thoughts, words, and actions with spiritual principles, a process in which I've been engaged now for more than forty years, and which I teach to others.

My guides refer to this process as "attunement," an alignment of our conscious minds with the spiritual essence of life. Attunement can be compared to learning to play our individual instruments in harmony with the whole orchestra. Spirit is unlimited; human beings are limited—partly due to our manifestation in physical form and partly as a result of our errors, wounds, and warped perceptions. Attunement is a process of synthesizing the experiences of the limited and the unlimited, and then integrating the awareness that emerges from that synthesis into our attitudes and actions. We can experience being Spirit and human, holding both realities simultaneously; within that consciousness, we can begin to ask, from a much more expanded perspective, "Given who I am and what's going on, what am I to do?"

The insights we receive through attunement take us deeper than our cultural conditioning, because they're informed not by preconceived notions but by universal principles and concepts that reside at the core of us all. We can begin to differentiate between destructive conditioning—the tacit agreements or explicit messages that confuse and limit our thinking and behavior—and messages that actually help us to actualize our true identities and the purpose of our current incarnation. For although we are all evolving toward actualizing our spiritual nature, even if it doesn't appear so, each of us has a purpose, which varies from person to person.

Through attunement, through choosing to connect and communicate with our own inner Spirit and the spiritual force all around us, we can start to experience that we are all interconnected and we are all individuals. We can develop the ability to understand our own individual roles, priorities, creative natures, and contributions, while respecting Oneness and interconnection. We become able to hold both of these perspectives simultaneously, and I must add that it feels good all over to achieve this state.

That said, attunement isn't something we accomplish once and then move on. It's a constant process of adjustment to the conditions in our lives as they are and as they continue to unfold—but from a spiritual perspective, in both perception and feelings. As a guide once said to me, "Not only do we attain, we sustain." In other words, there are no rules to memorize, no strict laws or commandments to follow. Attunement is the development of situational awareness, a continuing attentiveness to aligning with an evolutionary force that is much greater than any one of us. Nor is the development of this awareness a one-size-fits-all process. Attunement develops according to the particular complexity of each person's life.

FIRST CONTACT: MEDITATION

Attunement is like the hub of a wheel: There are numerous ways to access it, which I think of as spokes leading to the center. Many of the approaches and techniques don't require a significant investment of time and are easy to integrate into a busy life. But the first of these, meditation, involves stepping back from your customary routine and carving out a certain amount of time dedicated to practice. Whether you choose fifteen minutes or an hour, what is most important is the development of a habit. Meditation is an important skill, the ability to listen deeply. Through sustained, acute stillness, we can make contact with our inner Spirit and the greater Oneness that is all-encompassing. I introduce meditation in the very first session of the classes I teach, because it is the foundation on which other methods of attunement are built.

As with any skill, proficiency in meditation is developed through repetition. The more you meditate, the easier it becomes to enter and maintain internal tranquility. At some point, disengaging at will from ordinary mental busyness becomes as natural and as immediate as other skills you take for granted, and you'll be able to achieve a meditative state at any point during the ordinary course of the day. But first you need to train yourself to do it much as you trained yourself, say, to ride a bike or read a book.

The approach to meditation I teach differs from some other meditation practices popularized nowadays, in that it is an interactive process rather than a relaxation exercise. The method begins with stilling the mind, not as an end in itself, but as a means of opening ourselves to direct contact with our inner Spirit and with the force of Oneness. Through this communion, we can begin to transcend our conditioned perceptions and attain deeper insights for navigating our lives.

The meditation practice I first learned from my guides, which I teach to students and clients, uses the image of an X to symbolize the process. The bottom portion of the X represents our everyday "brain chatter," the flow of thoughts that ordinarily command our attention. The upper portion of the X represents our connection with the Spirit within and the Oneness—and sometimes, with spiritual guides. The central point at which the two sections of the X meet represents the threshold of stillness, where brain chatter ceases and we can begin to receive insights and revelations. The task of meditation is to reach the point of stillness and sustain it, opening the door to an expansion of perception.

The practice of sustained meditation involves three basic steps. The first step, omitted by many forms of meditation taught today, is to focus on something that inspires you. Inspiration is the way to cultivate an open, spacious sensation at the top of the head, a prerequisite to meditation. People familiar with the chakra system will recognize this description as an open crown chakra; the crown chakra is the door to that upper portion of the X, the bridge to direct spiritual experience. Others might recall Emily Dickinson's description of poetry: that it makes you feel as if the top of your head has come off. Dickinson was responding to the inspirational function of poetry, and inspiration is a wonderful and accessible means of initiating contact with the upper part of the X. Sources of inspiration are varied and numerous. For some, music may open this chakra; for others, recalling a moment of beauty, an experience of art, a passage in literature, a vista, or a memory of spending time in nature can trigger the sense of expansiveness.

The next step in sustained meditation is to still the mind, a process that can be facilitated by using a positive affirmative statement that helps you to focus your attention on a single thought while simultaneously cultivating a positive attitude. In my classes, I suggest using "I am Spirit, infinite Spirit," as a reminder that we are more than human. Any positive affirmative statement can be effective, though; like homeopathic remedies, some may be more effective for certain people than for others. For example, some people have had success affirming "I am" or "I am that I am."

After choosing an affirmation, repeat it silently in your mind or aloud until an expansive peaceful feeling grows, then pause and practice holding your mind still. In the beginning, brain chatter will likely start up again pretty quickly; when that happens, just go back to repeating the affirmation, then take a pause again. It's kind of like a rocking, a lilting sensation: repeating the affirmation and pausing; repeating the affirmation and pausing; repeating the affirmation and pausing. Gradually you'll be able to hold the pause longer and longer. Some days when you meditate, you'll find that you can hold your mind still more easily; other days you can't. So use the affirmation to help still the brain chatter, hold the pause, and make the pause longer as you can. If you need to use the affirmation a lot, that's fine.

Once you can hold your mind still for a sustained period of time, the final step is to let go of the affirmation and allow yourself to experience the upper part of the X, which is commonly felt as a deep sense of expansiveness and connection to something larger than your individual self. There are an infinite number of ways that this wide, wonderful feeling can manifest, depending on your particular situation. Some people may have a vision of green light, the color associated with physical healing; others will receive insight into a pressing concern; someone else may have a memory of a previous life. I often say that a deep meditation is better than going to the movies!

As a tool to prepare yourself for meditation, practice perceiving the Spirit in yourself and others during ordinary daily activities. When you're brushing your teeth, for example, look at yourself in the mirror and affirm, silently or aloud, "I am Spirit, infinite Spirit," while you aim the arrow of your consciousness right into your core. In the grocery store, when you are waiting in the checkout line, use the affirmation "I am Spirit, everyone is Spirit," as you gaze around at other people. Remembering that what you focus on is what you see, just let this be an experiment. Discover how your experience changes as you remember the Spirit in yourself and others.

There are other ways to activate connection with the experience of Oneness. Years ago, I lived in the country and we had a big, thirty-acre field. At times it was my turn to mow the field, going around and around on our Kubota tractor. At first I thought, "Okay, let's get done." Then I realized, "This is going to take a long time. I've got to get into it. I've got to let go of time and get into the flow." And in the midst of that feeling of being one with the sky and the grass and the birds, I'd find myself in a meditative state of stillness and connection. The same sort of state can be experienced, for example, by people who play golf or engage in some other activity that involves a good deal of focus and concentration. Immersed in the game or activity, they can attain a state of profound stillness and connection. Consciously or not, they're tapping into an experience of Oneness—a profoundly enjoyable, relaxed, and energized state that allows them to perform at their best.

Perhaps you're walking down a busy street with crowds of people around you. You're trying to get to a destination, and you're feeling disconnected, separate from all those other people and the traffic and so on. There are ways to practice connecting with the Oneness in that kind of situation. One way is to use one of my favorite affirmations: "I am Spirit temporarily on the earth. Everyone is Spirit temporarily on the earth." Another is the exercise I described earlier: looking at people with the intention to discern the Spirit beneath their appearance. When we place our attention on the spiritual essence in people, we start to be aware of it and feel connected. It's actually a remembrance that we are one and we are separate—and when we remember, we start to see. As my guides say, "Spiritual essence is always there, but you can't see it until you switch on your consciousness. It's just like walking into a darkened room full of furniture: All the furniture is there, but you can't see it until you switch on the light. Consciousness is the light switch on the wall."

CHAPTER THREE

The Human Condition

What does it mean to manifest true self?
What does it look like in your home, in your work,
in your body, in your relationships?

Many years ago, an incident occurred that caused me to feel betrayed by a friend. At the time, a journalist working for a local newspaper lived across the street from my house. My friend decided to tell this neighbor intimate details about my life without my permission—though with the pure, but misguided, intention of helping to promote my work. I first learned about this while reading the local newspaper, where I discovered an article about me. It was a shock, but I knew immediately what had happened. When my friend stopped by for a visit I confronted her, feeling so hurt and angry that I started to cry. As my tears flowed, a remarkable experience unfolded.

I became transfixed by a series of vivid visions, in the screen of my mind, of human suffering on a scale that completely surpassed my personal heartache.

I saw images of people who were starving and lonely; people mired in war; people who desperately wished for their lives to be different. The scenes flashed by, triggering my sobs and illuminating the enormous expanse of pain and suffering that has been, and continues to be, a part of the human experience. Occasionally the flow of visions would stop, allowing me to catch my breath, and then it would start up again, along with my tears.

The images included people throughout history and cultures from all over the world. I saw bodies piled up in carts during a time of plague, a child who died quietly in its grieving mother's arms, Chinese women and children being slaughtered by Mongolians on horses, families in conflict, and many visions of soldiers—young men not much older than boys—in the midst of combat. This emotional internal slide show went on for more than two hours, while my friend tried to comfort me.

I wept for the misery and anguish that humanity has endured through the ages, and for individual lives marked by brutality, grief, betrayal, and loss. I sobbed for my own sorrows, too, for they were also part of the tapestry of pain laid bare by my visions. As the experience continued, I began to feel a profound sense of union with the collective suffering that has characterized so much of our human experience.

Abruptly, the visions shifted to images of joy and celebration. I began to see groups of people laughing, dancing, and making music. I saw a woman giving birth. In great detail,

I saw people of different races, creeds, and cultures expressing love and generosity toward one another in a variety of ways, living in harmony with nature, and working together toward common goals, such as building a barn. All these images elicited more tears—but this time they were tears of joy.

When the visions finally stopped, I was left with a deep, abiding peace and an unshakable knowledge that we are more than human. Beneath the surface appearance of physical form, Spirit shines undimmed, as it always has. At the same time, I recognized the necessity of embracing, rather than avoiding, the full range of our human experience, of acknowledging and accepting the tragedies alongside the triumphs. In that moment, I knew I wanted to help alleviate suffering in our world, and I gave my compassion freely and completely to all people in all places.

It became clear to me that in order to accurately comprehend who we are, and our personal and collective evolution, we must experience both our nature as Spirit—which is our essence and potential—*and* its human expression, which reflects our stage of awareness and actualization on the earth at a particular time. Spirit is constant and clear. It inspires; it is infinitely wise, loving, creative, and compassionate. Human beings, by contrast, are complicated and usually reveal themselves only over time. Consider the many different thoughts, moods, feelings, interactions, and events each of us experiences over the course of a single day—or even a single hour. Think about the different selves we assume and present to others, the different roles we play in various situations. Bear in mind, too, that no two people experience the same thing in exactly the same way. Every minute of every day these experiences, thoughts, feelings, and so on arise and pass among the billions of people across the world. This complexity and variety constitute what my guides refer to as the "human condition."

HOW DID WE GET WHERE WE ARE?

You may wonder, if Spirit is the essence of all things and pervades all things, how can there be such complexity? How can there be any negativity?

A vision I was given many years ago showed me that at one point, we were all united in Oneness. We had no individuality, not even at the spiritual level. We were a unified force of consciousness. According to my guides, a pure and powerful desire to express and to create emerged from within this unified consciousness. This was the "first cause," an undeniable yearning that triggered an explosion of creativity, which scientists refer to as the "Big Bang." In meditation, I had a vision of this event; it appeared to me as a great, limitless ring of fire containing all of life, which then exploded, sending sparks in all directions, marking the beginning of creation and the emergence of individual facets of the Oneness.

Each spark of the Oneness is the Spirit within living beings. As discussed earlier, the soul is the container of that spark; it allows us to maintain our individuality and—as an expression of the creative power of Spirit—it evolves. At first, souls evolved at the etheric level of energy, but then gradually moved toward a denser, physical level. The physical world is Spirit's outermost reach of creative expression, yet it is still a vibrant manifestation of energy. Most of us know from high school science classes that every material thing is energy in motion, including our own bodies. Our arms, for example, aren't truly solid, even though they appear that way. However, the energy of the physical realm, including our bodies, moves at a slower rate than that of the etheric realm. This denser realm provides us with different types of creative opportunities—for instance, the ability to experience physical senses.

A common confusion for many souls manifesting in this world is that the material and spiritual realms don't function in an identical way. In the spiritual realm, individuals with similar attitudes and vibrations are drawn together. Beings who are more deeply connected to spiritual principles reside, for the most part, in the outer, or higher, realms, while those transfixed by negative attitudes inhabit the lower realms and experience far less light and joy. By contrast, in the material world beings of many different stages of spiritual development are all embodied together. Here on earth, we can have a saint and a murderer on the same bus. This mingling of individuals at different stages of development accounts for much of the complexity of the human condition.

The negativity we experience as individuals here on earth can be traced back to first errors—the disconnect from Oneness and spiritual principles that snowballs into unbalanced and self-defeating attitudes and behaviors. As these attitudes and behaviors accumulate, our perspective as human beings becomes limited. We lose sight of our fundamental nature as Spirit, as interconnected sparks of Oneness, and become enmeshed in and attached to our sense of individuality—from which a pervasive sense of dichotomy emerges, with tightly held perceptions of good and bad, right and wrong, winner and loser.

In the higher spiritual realms, there is no dichotomy; there is simply Oneness, which contains only attitudes based in spiritual principles. In the lower etheric realms and on earth, where dichotomy tends to dominate, we're inclined to compound negative patterns arising from our first errors by reacting when circumstances are not how we wish them to be. Even if we are balanced and wise, if we react emotionally to someone who is not, we become trapped in the imbalance of our reaction, no matter how justified we might be.

However, if we're able to acknowledge and accept the dichotomy of the human condition from the infinite view of spiritual consciousness, we can begin to let go of our habits of reaction. I've seen this transformation occur in many people. One of the most personally satisfying examples involved my daughter, who, because she was dyslexic, struggled in elementary school. Though she'd always demonstrated high intelligence, she fought to learn to read and write, while at the same time contending with the teasing of her classmates. Every attempt to move her to an alternative school or learning environment fell through. So I went into meditation to ask my guides to explain what was going on. I was shown a previous incarnation in which my daughter was a French magistrate who flaunted his intelligence by reading flamboyantly to the peasants under his watch. In that lifetime, my daughter maintained an attitude of superiority, without much compassion for the struggle of the people around her.

When I told her what I'd seen, she became angry and frustrated. "So in that life I was mean to them and in this life they're mean to me," she began. "And in the next life I'll be mean to them again . . . and it will go on forever."

"That's one option," I replied, "but there's another one. If, instead, you can feel compassion for the fact that your classmates don't really understand what it's like to be dyslexic, then you won't take their behavior personally, which will heal your hurt, and the chain of reaction will be broken."

My daughter's immediate response was simply to take in the conversation. I knew that learning to feel compassion, rather than the emotional hurt triggered by others' behavior, was a deep, lifelong lesson for my daughter—as it is for many—and that life would bring her this lesson many times. We've repeated the essence of this conversation through the years as my daughter has grown into a compassionate adult.

The point is that feeling and expressing spiritual principles—in other words, actualizing our spiritual nature—frees us from reaction and breaks the momentum of the karmic snowball. Through spiritual attunement, we can maintain our human individuality while retaining our connection to the principles of Oneness, loosening the grip of fear and turmoil that results from a perspective of dichotomy.

NOTHING IS IN ISOLATION

Of course, there are aspects of the human condition that everyone shares. We all feel hunger and thirst; we all bleed when we're cut. We all have weaknesses and strengths. And we all eventually drop our physical bodies and reenter the spiritual world when we die.

When I was twenty-two, I was given an opportunity to experience directly the lesson of human commonality. I'd been asked to speak in front of a large group—around a thousand people—for the very first time, and moments before I was to begin my talk, I suffered an attack of stage fright. I actually contemplated running to the ladies' room to hide. When it came time to step in front of the crowd, my guide whispered to me, "Imagine everyone in the audience is without their clothes." As I walked up to the podium, I pictured all the onlookers naked. Almost immediately, I relaxed and became quite comfortable onstage. I was able to feel that we are all human and that everyone has imperfections. I no longer felt I needed to be perfect; being myself was quite enough. I even told the audience what I was visualizing and why. Everyone laughed and relaxed with me, and I was able to speak without fear.

The common ground we share as human beings extends even more deeply to the energetic, spiritual level. To clarify, we know that our limbs aren't really solid or separate from the rest of our bodies; as mentioned earlier, they are fundamentally energy in motion. And we know that although the space around us looks like there's nothing in it, it's brimming with frequencies, vibrations, and energies that are constantly interacting in various ways. Even from a scientific perspective, we know that everything is connected. So the concept of unseen interconnections isn't really surprising. What I've learned from my guides, though, is that these vibrations, these energies, are unified at the spiritual level, as well as endowed with consciousness. The distinction we typically make between animate and inanimate forms reflects, to a certain extent, a limited or distorted view. People and animals do have individual souls and undergo the reincarnation process. My computer, though it doesn't have a soul, is nevertheless an expression of the creative aspect of Spirit; its vibration is still woven into the fabric of life, which pervades everything.

The concepts of Oneness and interconnection have been pointed out to me on a number of occasions, and in a variety of different ways. For example, many years ago, I was enjoying weeding my flower garden, immersed in the blissful feeling of a perfect summer day. Suddenly, a guide gently whispered to me, "The joy you are feeling is touching all of life." Up until that moment, I was simply enjoying a lovely day, but after my guide whispered to me I was flooded by the awareness that consciousness was all around me, even though I'd thought I was alone. As a result of this realization, I began to feel more responsibility for the nature of my thoughts and feelings. They weren't isolated, private events; rather, they were deeply intertwined, affecting and affected by everything around me—beyond even what my physical senses could perceive.

On another occasion, a guide told me, "Earth is your school. The evolution of consciousness is the most important aspect of life on your planet." After I heard this, I began to wonder: *What does the evolution of consciousness mean?* Over time, I've learned that it means maturing toward the ability to feel, express, and manifest our spiritual natures in everyday life. Personal development, I've come to see, doesn't occur in isolation, for we're all connected whether we like it or not. We're all here to learn to experience the spiritual principles inherent in the Oneness and our human individuality at the same time. Without attunement to Oneness, and the fundamental principles that hold life together, individual selfishness or self-denial dominates. Ultimately, these imbalances are not sustainable on our planet.

In fact, I believe our world's environmental challenges are begging us to pay attention to the essential spiritual lesson of interconnection. Nature's ecosystems have demonstrated over and over again the basic truth that everything is interrelated; if we continue to place our focus on superficial individual desires and fears without bearing in mind this truth, we'll all suffer the consequences.

THE CLEAN-DIRTY-ROT-RUST EXISTENCE

It takes a lot of work to be human; it requires maintenance. We all must, on some level, deal with what I call the "clean-dirty-rot-rust existence." Clean things get dirty, painted things rust, and food quickly spoils. All areas of our life need constant attention. Most of us would prefer to delegate the maintenance aspect of the human condition and focus on the "important" part. But I've been taught, and have learned through experience, that consciously participating in the clean-dirty-rot-rust, or maintenance, part of the human experience helps keep life in perspective and teaches us humility in the midst of striving for greatness.

In the spiritual realm, we enjoy a certain kind of ease. There, travel occurs at the speed of thought. So does manifestation: If we want to wear a blue shirt, we only need to think it and instantly we'll be wearing one. When immersed in a realm of pure positivity, we feel wonderful while just coasting along.

However, in the material world, where there is time and work to be done, personal effort is necessary in order to maintain and manifest our life. We can't just think an outfit into being; we have to exert ourselves even to get dressed in the morning. Part of the reason we come to the earth is to learn to work with and to embrace the effort required in maintaining and developing our bodies, our relationships, our homes, and all of the material things we've accumulated. My guides say this effort leads us toward personal attainment and the ability to actualize our spiritual nature even in the midst of adversity. Mastering life, they say, is the capacity to actualize our true nature whether we're in a supportive environment or not. Consistency is key. However, we have a cultural conditioning that encourages us to aspire to ease, which isn't always best for our development and the world at large.

For example, a client of mine inherited a huge sum of money, which radically changed her life. She and her husband hired people to do all their cleaning, someone else to manage all the cooking, and another person to pay the bills. However, during the warm-weather months, she and her family moved to their summer house, where their lives were simpler and progressed at a slower pace. There, my client did the cooking and cleaning. She was surprised to discover how much she enjoyed these daily tasks and realized that delegating all her personal chores had actually created a feeling of being disconnected.

Most cultures value and reward progress—such as writing a book or coming up with a new product—more highly than maintenance. Consequently, many people regard maintenance as something to delegate. If they need to engage in some sort of maintenance, it's not uncommon to resent it because it's taking valuable time away from "making progress."

I'm what I call a "shuffler"—as opposed to a zoomer—which means that I aspire to develop and improve all the many aspects of my life as I go about each day. This includes focusing on my career; taking care of my health, my relationships, and my home; and continuing spiritual development. It all goes together.

I believe that maintenance and progress are equally valuable. If fulfillment is based on the actualization of our spiritual nature, then the quality of our inner life is just as important as our choices and worldly contributions. Being in the flow of life means actualizing the feelings and qualities of our Spirit when we're alone washing the dishes or making the bed as well as when interacting with others at a job or family gathering. When I participate in the many aspects of daily maintenance, I'm simply taking responsibility for my mess, my life.

I often integrate my spiritual practice with chores, upkeep, and caring for my body. Through my many years of meditation, I've learned to clean the house in a meditative state, wash the dishes while communicating with my guides, visualize sending light to people when I run errands, and practice letting go of my attachments as I'm vacuuming. Integrating spiritual practice in the midst of daily living can antidote resentments triggered by the huge amount of effort needed to maintain an individual human life or family and transform mundane tasks into enjoyable activities.

While managing the human condition requires at least some degree of effort, the work involved can become gratifying and enlivening when infused with the feeling of connection with Spirit and its qualities. For instance, a number of years ago, I needed to fly to California for a work opportunity. A few days before I was to leave, I received a phone call—the gist of which was that if I interrupted my flight and stopped in Chicago for a few hours, I'd have a chance to meet several people who might be interesting to me. I knew that if I chose to stop in Chicago on my way to California I'd need to take a red-eye and stay up most of the night. I decided to meditate on my decision, because I felt torn. On the one hand, I wanted to go to Chicago; on the other, I don't do very well if I don't get a good night's sleep. In my meditation, I was told, "It is important that you go to Chicago and meet these people. We will carry you." I stopped in Chicago, stayed up all night, had breakfast at three o'clock in the morning, and discovered I wasn't at all tired! The force of Spirit had carried me, enabling me to accomplish more than what was normally conceivable for me. And as predicted, I established significant relationships with individuals who stimulated my growth and helped me to bring my work to a wider audience.

When we attune to and utilize our connection with Spirit, we become able to accomplish tasks and experience events that go beyond what seems humanly comfortable or even feasible. This expansion of our powers and abilities isn't just a phenomenon of the moment; it's a change in us, part of the process of human evolution. When Spirit infuses the effort that the human condition demands, that exertion can become more manageable and more attainable. This can even happen at an extreme level. For example, what appears to us as a miracle—often seen in the realm of healing—can become more available to everyone. My guides say, "As the Spirit is brought forth more fully into the human condition, the human condition evolves and changes, and as this happens, what is considered normal and natural will evolve and change, and what was once an effort will no longer be an effort."

A BROADER VISION

Although we share a common humanity, understanding this commonality is not enough to accurately comprehend someone we encounter. We need to see both that person's spiritual essence and the particulars of his or her human persona at the same time. The same holds true if we want to understand ourselves. We need to see our Spirit, which is our essence and potential, and the human expression, which is our stage of awareness and actualization at a given time. In other words, to live more fully and to realize our potential, we need to hold Spirit and the human condition in the same vision.

We can begin to appreciate embracing both Spirit and the human condition through an incident that Holocaust survivor Viktor Frankl recounts in his book *Man's Search for Meaning*. One day he walked into a hut in the concentration camp where he was being held, and saw a young woman who knew she was close to death. Yet, as they spoke, the woman seemed content, even cheerful. When he asked her why, she replied that she was actually thankful for her current situation, even though it was so bleak, because in her former life she was self-centered and didn't consider spiritual accomplishment important. Then she pointed out the window of the hut toward a tree, saying that the tree literally spoke to her about the eternal, enduring presence of life itself.

The context of this story set in a concentration camp during the Holocaust renders the account epically vivid and dramatic. But if we take the woman at her word, as Frankl appeared to do, we can see that her recognition of why she was going through that experience helped her to accept her situation and find joy in the spiritual process, no matter how terrible the circumstance. We can say she recognized the human condition of her life as well as the fact that she was Spirit. From a spiritual perspective, she saw beneath the surface of appearance to a deeper truth. Her testimony echoed the profound lesson that I'd first learned from my mother when she spoke to me after her physical death—that if you look deep enough, you will see that there is justice and a purpose.

A further detail regarding the experience I described in chapter one, about the Native American who spoke through me during a meditation session with friends, serves as an example for understanding this broader perspective. When the Native American departed my body, I remember feeling that he'd left me with a residue of his consciousness, which expanded my own spiritual perception. As I was fully returning to my body, I heard my neighbor yelling at her son, screaming at the top of her lungs. I'd spent many years working with children and always felt very protective of them, but in this instance, when I was filled with a profound awareness, I saw visions of the boy in a previous life as a thief and a shady character. I was able to recognize that his Spirit had incarnated into this less-than-ideal situation as an opportunity to learn about the ramifications of his past actions: to understand what it feels like to be mistreated, and to learn not to mistreat others.

In fact, only a few days later the boy came to our house to visit and tried to steal something that belonged to me. I reprimanded him with the awareness that I was teaching him an old and important lesson. Once again, I felt that if I looked deeply enough, I could see there are reasons why certain situations arise in particular ways.

As you may recall from chapter two, the soul retains the records and memories of all of our past-life patterns. When we reincarnate we are guided toward parents and circumstances that trigger these patterns in order to bring them to light, and to provide opportunities to learn the lessons we need to move forward in our evolution. Healing the soul of negative patterns allows our spiritual nature to fully actualize. As I look back on my interaction with my neighbor's son, I can see the intention of Spirit at work, bringing us together in a specific situation that would not only aid him in his own evolution but also reinforce my own sense of the wisdom of Spirit's design.

A QUESTION OF BALANCE

Perceiving the integration of Spirit and the human condition can help us understand how we might best support the growth of another. We are all multidimensional beings. People can be struggling emotionally and physically, and at the same time their Spirit will be brimming with joy and acceptance. Through cultivating the awareness that all people are Spirit and human, we can begin to discern a course of action that can help a person manifest his or her best self. The process is simple. As you go into meditation, you can begin a dialogue with Spirit, asking, "How can I help the human condition in this person to evolve and grow?"

Perhaps you feel a deep affinity with someone, yet that person's behavior may be unpleasant and hard to tolerate. For example, I once counseled a woman who was married to a man with a drinking problem. Her husband's spiritual essence was wonderful, of course, and a bond had been forged between this woman and this man through many lifetimes. However, in his current life many of his choices were not in harmony with his spiritual nature, and living with him was difficult and very disappointing for my client. As she learned to see and compare the difference between her husband's spiritual nature and his behavior, she began to experience that it was possible to love him deeply but simultaneously choose not to tolerate his actions. In meditation, she was able to listen deeply in order to discern whether it was appropriate to stay in the relationship and work on improving it, or leave to make a better life for herself.

To use another example, a dear friend of mine finds it easy to see the potential in people. Their inner spiritual essence just leaps to the forefront of her perception. It's actually not so uncommon for people to fall in love with potential, only to become disappointed by the reality that most people are not yet enlightened. Focusing solely on Spirit, which is always magnificent, does carry risks. Although everyone has a wonderful core, some people are damaged, confused, and downright cruel—even destructive.

On the other hand, if we focus only on the particulars of

the human condition and don't acknowledge the Spirit, we miss out on the expansive experience of life's deeper meaning and our own and others' individual potential. When we focus on the human aspect of a person, it's easy to find the appearance of dichotomy: strengths and weaknesses, vulnerabilities and aspirations. In fact, my guides have said that in order for individuality to exist people must have strengths and weakness, or else everyone would be identical. From a spiritual perspective individuality and Oneness can coexist.

When we focus on the Spirit and the human aspects of a person simultaneously, we can acknowledge the discrepancy between the inspiring character of his or her Spirit and the not yet fully actualized human self. This balanced synthesis of perception evokes compassion for people, as well as a profound respect and awe for the process of evolution, from which no one is exempt.

PRACTICING SYNTHESIS

"I love humanity; I just don't like people." I don't know if this quote has ever been attributed to any individual, but it's a very common sentiment. People often like the *concept* of other people, but tend to have great difficulty actually getting along with others—whether in the context of a family, or work, or a nation. When we concentrate both on people's human self and on their Spirit simultaneously, caring and consideration grow toward all individuals, including ourselves.

When I teach classes on Spirit, I ask people to sit opposite each other and say, "I am Spirit and you are Spirit." Because what we focus on is what we see, people start to perceive beyond appearance to essence, and they experience a deep sense of awe and connection. When I teach classes on the human condition, I ask people to pair up facing each other and say, "I am human and you are human." I ask them to really look at and experience that human level of vulnerability, pain, confusion, kindness, and so on. Sometimes they feel self-conscious and uncomfortable.

Finally, I ask them to start synthesizing both perceptions simultaneously, by saying, "I am Spirit and I am human. You are Spirit and you are human." Usually, when my students view the human level and the Spirit together, they experience the Spirit as being profoundly magnificent and emotionally inspiring, and they commonly perceive a significant difference between consciousness at the spiritual core, and the human level of awareness. This disparity is perceived as the cause of emotional pain, which arouses compassion for the whole journey of being alive.

You can train yourself in a similar way. Begin by using the affirmation "I am Spirit, infinite Spirit," which was introduced as part of the meditation instructions in chapter two. It's not necessary to be sitting in a quiet room entering meditation to start working with this practice. Instead try it during an ordinary daily activity; for instance, when you're washing your face. While looking in the mirror say, "I am Spirit," and take a few moments to experience looking beneath your appearance into your essence. Next affirm the statement "I am human," repeating it a few times, while focusing on the level of your appearance and daily concerns. For some people, what comes up might be "I wish my teeth were less crooked" or "I wish my nose were smaller."

In fact, a lot of different experiences can arise when you focus on your human aspect, because of the complexity of being human. Feelings of vulnerability or fear might surface: "At any moment something terrible could happen. . . . I'm not going to be here forever." You might experience an acute awareness of your ability to taste, to touch, to feel, to experience all your senses. A whole set of thoughts and feelings associated with the clean-dirty-rot-rust existence might come up for you: "I need to clean my house . . . go shopping . . . earn more money." You might find yourself immersed in some of the more positive aspects of the human condition: the love you feel for your partner, your parents, your children, your friends. As you draw attention to your human aspect, a sense of your own little world emerges, as well as a sense of commonality with other humans.

Finally, integrate the two, affirming, "I am Spirit and I am human." Notice how your experience and perceptions change. You can also practice expanding this integrated perspective to perceive the Spirit and the human condition when interacting with others in daily activities. Mentally affirm, "I am Spirit and human; you are Spirt and human," while directing your attention to this synthesis. Notice how your perceptions, feelings, and interactions change.

These exercises are designed to take a minimum amount of time, so they can be woven into the activities of everyday life. They can be practiced while you're walking down the street, taking a shower, having dinner with your family, or working in an office among colleagues. Over time, these practices will transform how you naturally perceive yourself, others, and your involvement in situations or activities. Our perceptions are powerful because they inform our feelings, and our feelings inform our actions. Additionally, the more we train ourselves to connect with the spiritual aspect of life, the easier it will become to attune with it.

SHIFTING PERSPECTIVE

A while back, my son made an interesting observation. "From the human perspective, the human condition is a tragedy," he said. "From a spiritual perspective, the human condition is really interesting."

This is an accurate assessment on so many levels. From a human perspective alone there does not appear to be justice—life is not fair, and there's an incredible amount of suffering. However, from a spiritual perspective, we all have a complex story with specific unfinished business to conduct with our pasts; wounds and fears to confront and resolve; and lessons to learn. As my guides continue to remind me, we have come to the earth to learn, to contribute, and also to enjoy the gift of the physical world. The human condition perceived from the infinite view of Oneness reveals that everyone is part of an interconnected whole, with each individual having a particular purpose and a part to play.

Recently, my good friend Richmond passed into the spiritual world at age ninety-two. He had lived a full life: first as a teacher, then as a headmaster, and later as a board member of many nonprofit organizations dedicated to serving children and preserving nature and the earth. He had requested that I speak at his memorial, in order to relay a message from him from the spiritual world to his family and friends. When I first heard of his request, I thought, "Oh my, I hope Richmond comes to me so I'll have something to say." I meditated on him and saw in my mind's eye that he was rejuvenating, and he was extremely curious to learn more about life from the new perspective death had brought him.

One evening a few days before his memorial, Richmond appeared to me while I was ironing. Surrounded by gold light, he was as tall and thin as he had been in his physical body, but now he looked much younger than when I had known him. He suggested that I get a pen to write down his message.

He said, "Life is more beautiful than I ever imagined. Life on earth is a school. Don't be confused by what you have been taught. Rather, close your eyes and listen closely to your inner resonance. Everyone must be courageous to follow a higher calling than society's prescription. I am no longer worried, for I now see a deeper truth."

The statement "I am no longer worried, for I now see a deeper truth" was the most powerful sentence for me, because Richmond had been extremely worried in his life—not for himself, but for the future of humanity. It now seemed that with his more expanded perception he could see life on earth in a larger context.

At the same time that I received Richmond's message, I had the feeling that he had brought me a gift, a little piece of heaven. I felt enveloped in bliss, a sense of all spiritual principles melded together in my consciousness. I maintained this intense warmth and joy, without interruption, for more than an hour.

But then my toast burned, my computer acted up, and gradually heaven began to fade. This is the challenge we all share. Our task here on earth and in the body is to learn to sustain the qualities of spiritual Oneness right in the middle of the human condition teeming with dichotomy.

CHAPTER FOUR

Deep Focus—
Activating the Third Eye

When you open two eyes, open three.

One of the simplest and most effective ways to experience the qualities of Oneness in the midst of the human condition is through deep focus, a form of concentration that gives us access to a level of wisdom and clarity that can protect us from becoming overwhelmed by our emotions or confused by the mixed messages of cultural conditioning.

A guide first helped me learn the power of focus and concentration one afternoon more than thirty years ago, while I was in the middle of a mundane task: my once-a-week major grocery shopping trip. My cart was full of all kinds of fresh produce and bulk items, but when I pushed the grocery cart through an aisle stocked with crackers, cookies, and other packaged baked goods, I suddenly started to feel chest pain and numbness. I panicked, afraid that I was having a heart attack and might die, leaving my small children without me to care for them. My fear wasn't totally unjustified: A few months earlier I'd been diagnosed with a floppy heart valve, but I hadn't yet learned that my condition wasn't serious.

As I struggled with emotional turmoil, everything around me became a blur. Then I heard a guide whisper, "Focus, focus. Read a label on a package or find a point to stare at. Focus, focus."

I grabbed a box of crackers and put my complete attention without interruption on reading the side of the box: *Ingredients . . . Whole grain rye flour, yeast, salt . . . product of Sweden . . .* all the nutritional facts, and on and on. Gradually, my mind stopped racing, I began to breathe more deeply, and my fear dissipated. When I was calm again my symptoms steadily subsided and I felt reasonably sure I wasn't having a heart attack. But the most amazing part of the entire episode was the discovery that I wasn't able to feel frightened and deeply focused at the same time. As I continued through the store filling up my cart, I practiced concentrating on a variety of labels and points and soon realized that any point of focus worked as well as another. For the first time I consciously experienced that the ability to genuinely focus and concentrate is an antidote for anxiety, and it simultaneously stimulates clarity. This was a revelation to me.

With the help of my guides, I learned that deep focus is appropriate and beneficial in all life circumstances. When we maintain focus, we can manage the ups and downs of life.

When we lose our focus, we can easily become emotionally overwhelmed.

For example, one spring evening a few years after the grocery store incident, I was getting ready to leave home to teach a meditation class when my son, who was about five years old at the time, threw a temper tantrum. As he lay on the floor angrily shouting about being left with a babysitter, I explained to him that I was going to teach a class and that I'd see him for breakfast in the morning. Then I asked the babysitter to get him interested in some activity, such as reading a book or building towers with blocks. I felt awful as I walked from the house to my car, and guilty about leaving my son when he was distressed, but I knew I had a responsibility to my students.

As I started driving down the hill leading away from my house, a guide gently said, "Focus on *points*—the end of a branch, the top of a post, the corner of a sign." This instruction wasn't unfamiliar to me. In preparing for the birth of my first child I'd learned the Lamaze method, which teaches the technique of focusing on a point during labor. I'd chosen the top of a pine tree outside my hospital window. When I aimed my attention at the tree during labor, I was able to manage the pain of my contractions. When I would lose my focus, I would become overpowered and scared by the pain. My guide's instruction was similar, except instead of aiming to alleviate or reduce physical pain, this exercise was intended to calm emotional turmoil.

After I focused on points for a while during my drive to class, my emotional balance returned and it became quite clear that my son was fine with his babysitter and that his mood would pass. My earlier uncertainty and anxiety were replaced with the confidence that teaching my meditation class was the appropriate action for all concerned. When I returned home, I learned that my son's tantrum had ended soon after I left, and he spent the rest of the evening drawing and playing games.

In retrospect, I realized that in following my guide's coaching, I was shifting my attention from the emotional center in my gut to the middle of my forehead. In fact, not long after the incident with my son, a guide told me while I was teaching an evening class, "When you open two eyes, open three." This was his way of introducing the concept of integrating the perception of sensory information received from our physical eyes with a broader, deeper mode of spiritual perception offered by the "third eye"—one of the most influential energy nodes of the chakra system, and the source of deep focus.

THE CHAKRAS

Some of you may already be familiar with the chakra system. For those who aren't, let me offer a few words of explanation. The chakra system exists in the aura, or human energy field, of every person, and consists of a series of centers that are aligned from the top of the head to the base of the spine. The word *chakra* means "wheel" in Sanskrit, and each center or wheel of energy embodies a different aspect of our character. Each chakra center serves in various ways to receive, emanate, and process our life experiences. This energetic system impacts our lives whether we are aware of it or not—just as human anatomy and physiology functioned before people understood the mechanics of the physical body.

I'd turned my attention to learning about the chakra system about ten years after my spiritual awakening. I was motivated by a desire to understand more fully the complexity of human behavior. In particular, I was puzzled by people who were adept and very mature in certain areas of their lives, but quite childish in others. I often call people with this pattern "PhD kindergarteners." I thought the chakra system might help me fathom the intricacy and multifaceted nature of people. At the time, I'd heard enough about it from a lecture I'd attended and from people around me who were interested in the topic to recognize that each center represents different aspects of our nature.

However, because my guides consistently stressed the importance of experiential knowing—and because descriptions and explanations of the chakra system vary among different spiritual traditions—my approach to learning about the chakras was to forgo reading on the subject. Instead, I chose to learn from my etheric teachers and use my clairvoyance to observe people's chakras directly in order to draw my own conclusions. I was particularly interested in how the chakras function in everyday life. I wanted to understand why a spiritually devoted person could be a poor parent, or why someone extremely wise in some areas would make unfortunate or inappropriate choices in others.

For many years I became a serious "chakra watcher," intent on identifying the attitudes and actions that support a healthy alignment of the qualities associated with each chakra and those that cause imbalances. My investigation has led me to understand the chakra system in the following way:

- **The Crown Chakra**, as mentioned in chapter two, is located at the top of the head. It's the center associated with trust, inspiration, spontaneity, and feelings of devotion. When the crown chakra is in a healthy state, it feels good to be alive. It's also the chakra that gives us access to the spiritual dimensions, which is why it's important to open our crown at the beginning of a meditation.

- **The Third Eye Chakra**, which is the main focus of this chapter, is located in the middle of the forehead. It's the center of focus and concentration, clarity of mind, clairvoyance, and the discerning wisdom that sees beneath surface appearances.

- **The Throat Chakra**, as the name implies, is located in the throat area, and is associated with confidence in one's own value, verbal expression, personal power, and our attitude toward learning.

- **The Heart Chakra**, located in the middle of the chest, is the energy center most closely associated with the experience and expression of love, generosity, joy, courage, and forgiveness.

- **The Solar Plexus Chakra**, located above the navel area, is the center of emotion and harmony and is associated with the feelings we commonly refer to as "gut reactions." This chakra is often most noticeable when activated by nervousness or anxiety, as the feeling of having "butterflies" in your stomach.

- **The Identity Chakra** is located at the midpoint between the ovaries in women or girls and in a similar area in men and boys. This is the chakra associated with one's persona in the world and in relationship to others; the balance between the receptive and directive principles—knowing when to wait and when to act; as well as individual creative expression and sexuality.

  The Base Chakra is located at the base of the spine. Its nature is order, discipline, responsibility, attention to detail, and comfort with one's body and on the earth.

Watching chakras and auras has taught me that most people tend either to rely on analytical thinking to navigate their lives, or to "follow their gut," allowing the solar plexus chakra to dictate their attitudes and behavior. My guides advise third eye perception as a more practical approach that enables us to perceive situations and make choices based on wisdom and discernment, while simultaneously steering our emotions and intellectual analysis.

I've also noticed that people's auras differ greatly depending on where they consciously or unconsciously place their attention. If they make decisions based on gut feelings alone, the energy of their aura concentrates in their solar plexus region. If the intellect dominates decision making, the auric energy concentrates at the side of a person's head, just above the ears. But when the third eye is activated, the entire aura brightens dramatically and expands in size, a reflection of the positive perspective of wisdom and a spiritual outlook.

ACTIVATING THE THIRD EYE

The third eye chakra is central to developing the skill of deep focus, and can be activated either through conscious choice or as a side effect of some other effort. Either way, it produces a mental state often referred to in sports as "the zone." In fact, many athletes speak freely about and accept the zone as a state of consciousness reached through complete absorption in the game or activity—a kind of beam of concentrated energy that dissolves self-consciousness and allows pure participation in the present moment. Although many aspire to master the zone, because of its advantage in achieving one's best performance, few seem to realize that the third eye is the key to actualizing this desired state.

Quite literally, focusing out of the middle of the forehead switches on the clear perception of the third eye. Almost immediately, anxiety over the outcome of a particular problem or challenge dissolves. Other people or environmental factors become less distracting and fear in general dissipates. As our thoughts and feelings are leavened by wisdom and positivity, confusion gives way to greater clarity and priorities become more obvious.

This may sound too good to be true, but let me share with you a simple story about my daughter. A number of years ago, when she was an adolescent and feeling emotionally distraught about school and her life, I asked her to stare at the flame of a candle. I explained to her that concentrating on the flame would switch on her third eye perception, allowing the wisest part of her to rise to conscious awareness. Once she focused, I advised her to ask herself questions; the insights she'd receive, I suggested, would very likely help resolve her turmoil. I don't re-member precisely what she asked, but I do recall the dramatic emotional change that followed. In that moment, my daughter transformed from being confused and utterly upset to ex-pressing a calmness and clarity that reminded me of a wise sage.

PRACTICING THIRD EYE PERCEPTION

After several years as a teacher and clairvoyant counselor, I began experimenting with teaching a method of comparing perception filtered through the solar plexus and perception focused out of the third eye. Time and again, I'd see students and clients startled and thrilled to discover significant positive change in their experience, insight, and perspective. Someone confused and nervous while focused in the solar plexus would become more sharply perceptive and emotionally stable when focused through the third eye. Someone seething with anger after an argument with a friend or spouse, for instance, would feel the anger dissipate after seeing the situation through the third eye, replaced by deeper understanding of the specific circumstance and clarity about the next steps to be taken.

These experiences validated my guides' instruction. Anyone who could gently raise her focus to the middle of her forehead and hold her attention there experienced a remarkable change in attitude. A friend of mine named this method of comparing perception from the solar plexus to perception through the third eye the Tadd Technique.

Acquiring proficiency in deep focus and third eye per-ception requires practice and repetition. The instructions I developed in teaching clients and students are quite simple and straightforward: Sit up straight with your spine aligned and rest your hands comfortably on your thighs, palms down. Close your eyes, focus from your solar plexus, and imagine yourself late for an important appointment. Be aware of what you feel and what you do in such a situation. Make a mental note of your response. When you're finished, put your palms up and rest them on your thighs.

Now, while you remain sitting with your eyes closed, tap the point in the middle of your forehead. Many people believe the third eye is located between the eyebrows, but it's actually in the midpoint of the forehead, between the eyebrows and the hairline. Tap that point, so you'll know where to aim your attention, and then gently draw your focus to that location, keeping your eyes closed. Imagine the same scenario, being late for an important appointment, but this time focus through the point at the middle of your forehead. Notice the difference in your feelings, perceptions, and how you go forward in that situation.

Usually, this brief exercise convincingly demonstrates that a simple shift in focus can profoundly alter the quality of our experience and observations. While focused in the solar plexus chakra, it's quite common to feel anxious and rushed. By contrast, third eye perception as a rule generates relief from stress and a proper perspective. Being late is not usually a big deal in the scheme of life. When we can accept that, we're better able to make wise decisions and take appropriate actions to respond to the situation.

After working with the first exercise, try one that is more emotionally challenging. Sit up straight with your palms on your thighs, close your eyes again, and recall a conflict with a family member. Visualize this memory and feel it in the solar plexus region. Be aware of what you feel, what the other person feels, the relationship between the two of you, and how you wish to go forward with the relationship. Make a mental note of your experience.

When you're finished, turn your palms up. While keeping your eyes closed, raise your focus once more to the middle of your forehead. Tap this point with your index finger for just a moment to reinforce third eye focus. As you reexamine the situation through your third eye, observe the difference in your emotional state and outlook.

More than likely, you'll see for yourself that when your perception is filtered through the solar plexus, you're more likely to be emotionally reactive, perhaps intensely so. Your reaction may be one of anger, frustration, or emotional hurt. When the solar plexus chakra dominates, most people are unable to understand the other person's point of view. Dissimilar perspectives are often taken as an affront. The tendency in such cases is to respond in a way that escalates conflict.

Third eye perception is more objective and allows us to see with deeper clarity what is really going on. It embraces the possibility that our thoughts and feelings have become rigid, that we may have become too strict in determining what is "correct" or "appropriate." It allows us to learn more readily from others, even those with whom we disagree.

PRACTICAL AND PROFOUND

I call the third eye chakra the "kingpin" of the chakra system, because the clarity of third eye perception can transform our lives in profound and practical ways. In situations in which we're nervous, perceiving through the third eye can help us to stay calm and attuned to our inner wisdom. For example, when we enter a room or meeting filled with people who might have strong opinions or emotional confusion, staying focused through our third eye helps us remain centered. From that state of composed clarity, we become positive influences and contributors, rather than casualties of a chaotic environment. Maintaining our own concentration enables us to hold on to our identity and our priorities; we're less susceptible to being pulled out of balance and at the same time we can remain open and receptive to learning from others.

My guides refer to the third eye chakra as the miner's light on the forehead, because it illuminates each individual's path in the midst of life's confusion and complexity. Because the third eye generates a spiritually attuned view, decisions made from this point of focus are appropriate for everyone.

When groups of people come together to try to resolve a common problem, third eye perception enables everyone to move beyond their personal agendas to a broad perspective that can include the entire group. To use an example, I recently taught a class of about thirty people of varying ages and backgrounds how to reach consensus in a group when people have very different perceptions and objectives. First, we discussed a topic: the heated political issue of whether or not it was appropriate for the magazine *Charlie Hebdo* to feature a front-page image of Mohammed crying. I knew this topic would generate a debate involving different points of view, which is what happened. After our discussion, I asked everyone to meditate, to still their brain chatter and put aside their preconceived notions, while focusing out of the middle of their foreheads. Once they were in deep concentration, I asked them to turn their attention back to the political question. To their amazement, many changed their viewpoint.

Describing the experience, one woman in the class said, "Before I looked through the third eye, I saw the situation from my perspective and thought the image was a very positive thing, because it appropriately portrayed Mohammed as sad about the current conflicts and violence. But then, through my third eye, I was able to appreciate a Muslim perspective— one of believing that it isn't proper and fitting to depict the image of Mohammed. This insight helped me to see that the magazine cover was antagonistic in the midst of a volatile situation."

PERCEPTION INFORMS FEELINGS

One of the most important lessons my guides taught me early on was that perception informs feelings. When we approach a situation from either the intellect or emotions alone, we're more likely to interpret that situation from a biased point of view based on our past personal experiences. But when we engage the third eye, we move into an objectivity that takes us deeper than a self-centered view. A situation that may make us angry when seen from one perspective shifts into greater openness and understanding. Third eye perception stimulates a spiritual outlook, which my guides often refer to as wisdom.

It's important to understand the difference between a

developed intellect and wisdom. Most people have the capacity for analytical or intelligent thought, which can be highly refined through education; however, a developed intellect doesn't necessarily equate with wisdom. Wisdom is the ability to recognize the impact of conduct and its far-reaching effects, which in turn promotes sound judgment. Reliance on the third eye allows us to use our intellect as it's intended: as a tool for acquiring knowledge, understanding facts, and assimilating information, but not as an instrument for dominating perception. When people regard the intellect as the ultimate basis for judgment and interpretation, they often marshal selected facts to argue for their particular point of view. Discussions tend to turn into debates, in which the individuals involved use the facts and information they deem appropriate for making a persuasive case for whatever ideas they're advancing. Individual agendas rule, rather than the clarity and objectivity that come with the perspective of the third eye.

For instance, one of my clients had a tendency to ask other people what she should do when attempting to make a decision, because she struggled with a fear of making mistakes. She would go from one person to the next getting their opinions, becoming confused and often more afraid when her friends or family members offered different conclusions. I suggested that she look at the corner of a picture frame in my office, in order to activate her third eye. To her surprise, when she focused deeply on a point, she found herself capable of making decisions with greater ease and without so much fear. Eventually, she realized that she didn't need to rely on focal points in my office, for any point worked equally well.

THE THIRD EYE AND EMOTIONS

People sometimes wonder whether third eye perception inhibits our ability to experience emotions. I've seen in my work with clients and students that the third eye doesn't suppress emotions, but it does transform them. Emotional repression actually occurs when our perceptions are habitually weighed down by the energy of accumulated emotional baggage in the solar plexus. People who consistently process their experiences through their gut can become emotionally overwhelmed, turning into emotional sponges, arbitrarily absorbing the energy of their environments and the emotions of others. Consequently, the solar plexus chakra becomes dangerously enlarged, frequently causing people to resort to emotional repression as a form of self-protection.

By contrast, third eye perception serves as a filter to distinguish priorities from distractions and clarity from confusion. This refinement of perception helps us to make informed judgments and thereby take appropriate and protective actions, while preventing repressive and reactionary behavior. For example, when my son left home for college, I was guided to sell my house in the country, and move into Boston. I'd always lived in the country and the idea of following this guidance made me very nervous; I worried I might be making a big mistake. My guides had always stressed that I take their advice into myself for final confirmation, because this was my life, after all, and ultimately choices and responsibility were mine. So I used the Tadd Technique for myself in order to gain clarity.

When looking at this decision from my solar plexus, I just wanted to cry; the idea of making such a radical change seemed dreadful. Why would I want to live in a crowded, noisy, dirty city, when I could live near nature? But when I viewed the decision through my third eye, my attitude shifted dramatically. Moving to Boston felt completely appropriate, even if it meant selling a three-bedroom house in order to buy a small condo. As it ended up, my third eye was able to comprehend beyond my then-current level of awareness into the future, when my perspective would change. Boston offered me much more than my preconceived notions could have predicted. I became involved in the city's real estate market, which has brought me financial security; I met lovely, interesting people and discovered a variety of professional and creative opportunities. I also find the beauty of the architecture in my neighborhood endlessly inspiring. Now I can clearly see the wisdom in this decision; my third eye knew all along.

We often hear people advised to follow their gut—to make decisions from a perspective dominated by the solar plexus chakra. My guides consistently refute this suggestion, and my own experience in working with others confirms their wisdom. A few years ago, for instance, I gave a lecture to a large group mostly comprising high school students. During my talk, I taught the Tadd Technique, asking the audience to focus in the solar plexus while considering an important decision. Next, I had them compare their perceptions and conclusions from the third eye. After the lecture, a lovely young African-American man with dreadlocks and very baggy pants came up to me to say that when he tried to make his decision while focused in the solar plexus he felt very angry about a situation he'd found himself in and didn't know what to do. He didn't disclose any details, and inquiring would have been intrusive in this case, but he was visibly astonished by the change his third eye brought him. When he'd focused through the third eye, he told me, he simply felt no anger—only clarity. In amazement, he repeated a number of times, "When I was in the third eye, I wasn't angry!"

To use another example, when I lived on a dead-end dirt road in the country, one of my neighbors was a psychiatrist who professed to practice Buddhism. One day, as I looked across the road from my house to his, I noticed a young man I didn't recognize backing my neighbor's car out of the driveway. Suddenly there was a crash as he collided with a stone wall, denting the bumper of the car. My neighbor must have heard or seen the incident from his window. He ran outside screaming at the top of his lungs, "You idiot!" This was definitely a solar plexus reaction. My neighbor certainly didn't repress his anger; he let it all out, shocking and frightening the young driver.

It's actually very common to react with anger to unwanted or distressing situations when our attention is unconsciously focused in the solar plexus. Had my neighbor been able to perceive the accident through his third eye, he likely wouldn't have been happy about it, but he wouldn't have been enraged. Instead, he would have grasped that in the broader scheme of life the little accident wasn't such a big deal. The third eye gives us a proper perspective.

We're a solar plexus–dominant culture, though. Not long ago, I found myself in the midst of a Red Sox victory parade celebrating their World Series win. I hadn't actually planned to go, but we live only two blocks away from the parade route. I stepped outside our building and walked into a massive throng of people; millions were expected to turn out for this rolling rally. Horns blared, confetti flew, and elated fans screamed as the team members passed by in duck boats. The woman next to me was crying, and a group of teenagers nearby were blowing horns and cheering. All around me, people were expressing very strong emotions. I couldn't understand why this enormous crowd was so deeply emotionally invested in their home team winning. Then it occurred to me that I was observing the release of emotions built up in the solar plexus.

I found the scene fascinating, in part because a few days earlier I'd taught a workshop during which a number of people hadn't been able to manage the shift to their third eye until they'd experienced some type of emotional release in their solar plexus chakra. At the parade, I watched people's chakras—as I often do—and noticed emotional blocks and tensions being discharged and cleared through yelling, singing, or crying, because the spectators were identifying with being part of the winning group. The Red Sox victory helped people let go of personal anxieties and accumulated emotional strains held in their solar plexus chakras because they were happy to be getting something they really wanted: a World Series win.

When, consciously or unconsciously, we live our lives focused in the solar plexus chakra, emotional harmony becomes defined in terms of how we want things to be. If our desires are met, we're happy; if they're not, we're unhappy. We become dependent on outcomes, which makes us vulnerable to becoming victims of circumstance. In such a state, life can become a roller coaster ride.

I don't mean to suggest that the solar plexus is a "bad" center; only that it's often misused as the center of perception, rather than the center of emotion. A good analogy would be trying to use our mouths to see. Each body part has its appropriate role, as does each chakra. When misused, the solar plexus presents a significant common problem: the tendency to accumulate unexpressed emotion. If someone feels angry but doesn't express it, the anger collects in the solar plexus. Though it may be consciously forgotten, the anger forms an energetic block in this chakra, making it difficult to lift focus to the third eye. In fact, all emotional repression builds up in the solar plexus, forming blockages.

I'm not advocating that we express all our negative emotions all the time in order to keep the solar plexus healthy; quite the contrary. People are often amazed that a simple shift in focus can transform their emotional state. Third eye perception transforms our negative emotions into feelings based in spiritual principles, which are always positive: the feeling that the glass is half full instead of half empty. This positivity protects the solar plexus from becoming overloaded.

Sometimes, instead of following their gut, people are advised to "follow their heart." This was the case of one of my clients, a lovely and talented woman whose "heart" told her she was unhappy at work, so she quit her job and joined a meditation retreat center, expecting she would figure out a new, more satisfying way to live. But that didn't happen, and she depleted her savings and eventually lost her home.

"What went wrong?" she asked, bewildered, in my session room.

"The heart," I explained, "is like the sun. It's a radiator, not a discriminator. The heart is the center of love, while the third eye gives us the capacity for discernment that allows us to know how to express our love appropriately."

The message from her heart wasn't wrong, but she needed the tool of the third eye to help her navigate the details. Unfortunately for her, there was no simple resolution to the situation in which she'd found herself; only hard work enabled her to regain financial stability.

THE BENEFITS OF
THIRD EYE PERCEPTION

A friend who is a pilot explains that when he's flying through clouds, thousands of feet above ground, the sensations of ascending and descending aren't necessarily accurate, and relying on those perceptions alone can be catastrophic. "Don't follow what you feel; follow the instruments" is one of the first lessons of flight training. In fact, some pilots go so far as to say, "The instruments are God."

Third eye focus is a kind of "life instrument" to chart our course through the fluctuations of living; in some circles it's called the God's Eye. My guides' instruction "When you open two eyes, open three" is all about integrating a spiritual awareness into our daily living. Accordingly, the first thing I do upon waking in the morning is to stare at a point—usually the corner of a picture frame or window jamb—to activate my third eye. Then I ask, "What are my priorities today?"

Many years ago a guide said to me, "Put on your horse blinders and walk your path." It was his way of saying, "Don't get distracted." On a daily basis, most of us are confronted by so many distractions: other people's emotions and behaviors; the media; a tremendous amount to read, watch, and do. The sheer variety of choices available to us can be overwhelming, making us feel scattered. The challenge is compounded by our personal, interior distractions, the fears, uncertainties, and worries we carry around in our minds. There's only so much time in a day, and distractions from our purpose can eat up that time. Focusing out of the third eye while asking, "What are my priorities today?" helps us to stay on course.

When I watch spectator sports on television—whether it's baseball, Olympic skating, or golf—it's clear to me that when athletes are consciously or unconsciously focused in the third eye, their performance is well executed. When they're focused in their solar plexus, their performance is often disappointing, marred by mistakes. This principle applies not only to sports but to all types of performances or work projects: musical presentations, lectures, classroom teaching, and so on. I worked for a number of years with a professional clarinetist who struggled with performance anxiety. She was particularly nervous when playing as a member of an orchestra, her anxiety heightened by the pressure of other musicians' expectations. In my office, we walked through the solar plexus/third eye exercise so she could see the contrast for herself. Her disciplined nature served her well in learning third eye focus, which helped her not only to move out of fear into the joy of sharing the music but also to gauge how much preparation she needed for each performance.

Such examples illustrate how focusing through the third eye significantly supports our ability to actualize our potential. We all naturally shift in and out of the third eye;

however, when its influence is understood and intentionally applied, we're able to consciously choose clarity to navigate our lives.

WHY ISN'T THIRD EYE PERCEPTION MORE COMMON?

Some people find it difficult to look through the third eye. Years of regret, self-recrimination, guilt, and so forth can weigh us down like an anchor. Even if we try to bring our focus up to the third eye, the accumulation of unresolved emotional issues can pull it down to the solar plexus.

Holding unexpressed emotions in the solar plexus is an extremely common habit; in fact, everyone I know has this tendency in varying degrees. A particularly poignant case involved a man who attended one of my workshops. I was teaching the Tadd Technique and he just wasn't getting it. To help him, I used my clairvoyance to see what was going on in his solar plexus. As I talked with him about his blocked emotions, a long-buried memory came to the surface. He'd grown up in Ireland, in a family so poor they rationed their food so there would be enough for everyone to eat each day. One night after everyone was in bed, he gave in to temptation and snuck downstairs to the kitchen to eat some bread to quell his hunger. For decades, he carried unresolved guilt and shame around this incident in his solar plexus. As soon as this memory was raised to consciousness, he welled up with compassion for his younger self; relieved of the burden of guilt and shame, he was then able to access his third eye.

The more we practice looking at past situations though

the third eye, the more quickly we release old emotional blocks residing in the solar plexus. Conversely, the more we resolve emotional issues lodged in the solar plexus, the easier it is to sustain third eye focus in all situations. I always say, "You can go in the front door or you can go in the back door." Either way, third eye focus helps heal emotional confusion that can cloud and limit perception—which in turn facilitates the alignment of our conscious mind with Spirit.

LEARNING TO LET GO

When students have trouble activating the third eye, I suggest that they practice letting go of attachments in order to release the emotional baggage energetically anchoring them in the solar plexus. My guides define an attachment as a desire mixed with fear.

For example, one of my clients sought guidance about her adult son, who had mismanaged his financial affairs, resulting in significant credit card debt. When she attempted to look at the situation from her third eye, she simply couldn't get there. Her attachment to her son's well-being and her confusion about an appropriate response kept her stuck in turmoil. So I taught her my technique for letting go of attachments to support her ability to achieve enough inner calm that she could then access her third eye.

Like just about everything else worthwhile, the process of letting go of attachments can be developed through intention, focus, and training. I started letting go of my attachments during my daily three-mile walks. I'd focus on one possession, person, or place at a time. As I walked, I'd visualize pulling fears and attachments out of my solar plexus, while affirming, "I let go." If I discovered a feeling of resistance, then I knew this was an area that required more work.

To my surprise, as I let my attachments go, my perceptions sharpened: I felt more pleasure in daily living, and the love I felt intensified. I started to understand my guides' distinction between an attachment and an aspiration. An attachment, they explained, contains fear, while an aspiration is a pure desire, uncontaminated by fear. Essentially, in my practice, I was letting go of the fear of loss, rather than actually giving up a possession or my connection to a person or place. When our fears are released, our happiness and clarity increase. I started to learn what it was like to aspire to certain things, situations, or relationships without being burdened by fear.

For example, many years ago I went outside for a run, only to discover that I was overdressed for the weather, so I left my hat on a stone wall near my house as I took off down the road. When I returned, I saw a neighbor's dog with my hat hanging out of his mouth. We had a bit of a tug-of-war, which ended with me holding the tattered hat in my hand. I felt sickened— boy, was I attached. It was my favorite hat, a kind of an ap- pendage in cold weather, and I couldn't shake the feeling of regret and loss. Whenever I saw anyone wearing a hat, I missed mine. I tried buying hats that were similar, but none of them inspired me. So I decided to use the practice of letting go by visualizing my hat floating up into the infinite sky while I re- peated, "I let go." I continued this exercise for several months— while in the shower, stuck in traffic, or on my daily walks—until my regret was completely gone. After all my emotional angst had been released, I passed a store window in New York City displaying a dozen hats just like mine, in a variety of colors. Of course, I bought a bunch of them, but with a deep appreciation for the lesson of letting go of attachments.

The story of my hat illustrates an important principle: When you let go of anything that is meant to be yours, it *will* come back. When fears and attachments are released, barriers to manifesting what is meant to be are eliminated and our lives are able to flow in harmony with spiritual attunement.

I once had a client who experienced this principle in a relationship. She'd struggled with letting go of an intimate relationship that had ended. Years went by before she stopped feeling turmoil. When she finally accepted the situation and found peace, the man from her past—amazingly—called. He was ready to renew their relationship.

People are often afraid to let go because of the confusion about what it actually means. Too often it is believed that letting go means giving up hope. On the contrary, it signifies trusting life. I've been taught and have learned the hard way that the probability of manifesting our desires is much greater when we trust rather than fear.

INTEGRATING THIRD EYE PERCEPTION: A DAILY PRACTICE

It's possible to practice focusing through the third eye without closing your physical eyes or staring fixedly at a point, as my guide had first instructed me. Keep your eyes open while drawing your attention to the point in the middle of your forehead. At first, it might feel a bit awkward, like looking out of a triangle of three eyes. But with practice it begins to feel quite pleasant and natural, and it's common to experience a sensation of expansion and lightness. Actually, any activity that relies on focus and concentration—such as a sport, photography, flying an airplane, playing a musical instrument, or being deeply engrossed in reading—strengthens the third eye.

Practicing third eye perception with your physical eyes open also incorporates clarity into daily living. Try the Tadd Technique with your eyes open. Sitting comfortably, look around the room you're in while focusing your attention in the solar plexus chakra. Be aware of what you feel and your relationship to your environment. After you've spent a few moments doing that, bring your focus up and perceive out of three eyes: your two physical eyes and the focal point in the middle of your forehead. If you have difficulty, find an external point to focus on. Observe the difference in your feelings and perceptions. If you're like many of my clients and students, when focusing though your third eye you'll feel more optimism, greater clarity, and a deeper awareness of interconnection.

In addition, notice what you do with your focus throughout the day. Are you living from your solar plexus, driving your life with your analytical mind, or engaging the wisdom of the third eye chakra? You can shift at any moment. My guides say, "A spiritual perspective is just a pivot away."

When my son was in graduate school and living in the Boston area, he decided to try a third eye experiment. He resolved to make a concerted effort to maintain third eye focus for an entire day to see what would happen. In recounting this story, he told me that when he walked past a bus stop while focusing through his third eye, he felt a strong inner prompting to get on the bus. He boarded and rode until the bus stopped at the Boston Public Library, at which point he heard, "Get off the bus," in a distinct thought. He followed that guidance, and as he walked up the library stairs, he noticed an older Chinese man standing at the top. My son greeted him in Mandarin— a language he'd studied in high school and college—and they struck up a conversation. The Chinese man didn't speak English and was overjoyed to find someone to talk with. He'd come to the United States to teach calligraphy, he explained, but had somehow become separated from his translator and didn't know what to do. My son offered to act as the translator for his calligraphy classes, which turned out to be a blessing for this man and an interesting adventure for my son.

Using the deep focus that comes from third eye perception in that instance, my son experienced what my guides refer to as "maintaining the infinite view of Oneness-consciousness" in the midst of living in the human condition. They emphasize that making decisions from this clear, expanded perspective benefits everyone involved. What's more, third eye perception can be trained, directed, and projected, triggering a heightened clarity that allows us to perceive beyond appearances and culturally ingrained ideas.

CHAPTER FIVE

Working with Consciousness

Consciousness is like a rubber band
that can be stretched in all directions.

Several years ago, when my older brother was dying, I knew he was struggling with fear and uncertainty. To reassure him that death is not an end, but a continuation of life, I shared many of my guides' teachings, as well as a number of my personal visions and experiences. I explained to him that in the spiritual realm, thought is the mode of travel and communication, and the approach to manifestation. I suggested he think about his favorite self-image, because the thoughts we hold about ourselves manifest once we return to the spiritual realm. I knew he'd followed my advice when, twelve hours after his passing, he appeared to me in etheric form looking the way I remembered him as a college freshman.

Time doesn't exist in the spiritual realm as it does on earth; consequently, thought in the nonphysical world has an immediate impact. The denser vibrational environment of the physical world is also influenced by our thoughts, though the effects tend to manifest and become noticeable more slowly. Yet even in the material world, consistency in thought and visualization can exert great power in determining the direction of our lives. This is an important principle to consider as we examine three related skills: holding focus, expanding perception, and projecting consciousness.

THE POWER OF HOLDING FOCUS

Most of us have been taught to analyze or reflect on situations by moving from one thought to the next. Few of us have been trained to concentrate without interruption for a sustained period while focused on a single image or concept. As a result, when attempting to harness thoughts and images in order to seek insight or guide events toward a particular outcome, many people struggle with distraction. Yet the ability to hold focus and concentration is a remarkably versatile skill. As a friend once said, "It's like a Swiss Army knife, with a hundred and one uses and purposes."

Two incidents in my personal life vividly illustrate the power of holding a focus. The first, which occurred many years ago, involved my daughter's cat, Nitty—a name that came about because my young son wasn't able to say *kitty*. Nitty went missing for almost two days, so my daughter formed a search party consisting of herself, her brother, me, and a family friend, to explore the woods near our house. After a while, one of us heard Nitty crying, looked up, and saw him sitting on the branch of a pine tree at least twenty feet above the ground, clearly too frightened to find his way down. We didn't have a ladder tall enough to reach him, nor did any of the friends I contacted for help. I phoned our local fire department for assistance, but was told that more firemen were hurt rescuing cats than putting out fires, so they no longer offered that service.

We discussed what to do, and when no obvious solution presented itself I suggested we manifest a ladder through visualization. What other choice did we have? All four of us stood holding hands in a circle near the pine tree, and with our eyes closed, we held in our minds the image of a tall ladder leaning against the tree. Remarkably, within about fifteen minutes, we heard the roar of a truck coming up our dirt road. As it swung into view, we saw it was a telephone repair truck with a large yellow extension ladder hanging on a rack. Overjoyed, we flagged down the driver and when he stopped, we explained our dilemma. A kind young man, he told us that he'd be happy to help. He trudged through the woods with the extension ladder, leaned it against the pine tree, and expanded it to its maximum length—replicating our vision. Then he quickly climbed to our cat's rescue and brought Nitty safely back to my daughter's arms. Afterward, he told us he had telephone repair work to do on a nearby street, but *something* had compelled him to turn up our road.

The second story has a somewhat bittersweet ending. In 1983, while our former home was under construction, I decided I wanted a Jenn-Air stove for the kitchen. At the time, our budget wasn't large enough to include the eleven-hundred-dollar purchase. Using a magazine photograph as an aid, I started visualizing the image of the Jenn-Air stove in my new kitchen, with the conviction that somehow, when the kitchen was complete, that stove would be there. Every time I walked into the space that would become the kitchen, I pictured the four burners with the signature Jenn-Air rectangular exhaust vent in the middle of the stove. After about two weeks of "creative envisioning," I came across a classified ad in the local newspaper for a used Jenn-Air stove for three hundred dollars—a fraction of the cost of a new one. I bought it and had it installed. But once I started using it, I was disappointed to find it extremely difficult to clean. That experience taught me to tread a bit more cautiously when manifesting. As the old saying goes, "Be careful what you ask for, because you just might get it."

POSITIVE AND NEGATIVE

Both of these experiences confirmed an important principle my guides introduced early in my training: "Focus and concentration are equal to power." At its deepest level, holding focus brings us into contact with Spirit and its qualities, often in extraordinary ways. For example, my friend Henry, an elementary school speech therapist for many years, displayed a powerful healing ability starting at the age of sixty. When he began to feel comfortable publicly disclosing and demonstrating his gift, some of the faculty and administrators at his school became interested, lining up at his office door after hours to receive healings. While holding his focus on Oneness, Henry would put his hands on one person with a headache, another with arthritis, and then someone else suffering from asthma. Many people improved, and some were completely healed.

Henry knew his healing ability was directly linked to his capacity to hold his focus and concentrate. To keep his skill sharp, he practiced a variety of unusual focus exercises throughout his day. The one that stands out in my memory is his daily habit of using thought to evaporate the water on his body after his morning shower, instead of drying off with a towel.

Focus and concentration can be directed in either positive or negative ways. For instance, the stress of worrying about our own health or the health of a loved one can actually contribute to physical problems. My guides say, "Disease comes from attitude, environment, and karma."

Similarly, constantly dwelling on a person's negative behaviors can be a factor in reinforcing those traits. "If you want to support people in becoming their best self," my guides say, "hold the mental image of them as their best self." When my children were young, for example, my guides taught me to hold in the forefront of my mind thoughts and images of the preeminent qualities of their Spirit, as a way of helping them actualize their potential. The value of this advice became exceptionally clear when my son started school. In his first-grade class, the children who learned to read early on were often seen as the "smart ones," by both the teachers and the other children. This judgment—sometimes explicit, though more often left unspoken—helped those labeled the "smart ones" to excel and to become confident and therefore more receptive to learning, while the children who learned to read more slowly tended to be held in less regard, which contributed to their low self-esteem and difficulties in school.

From a third-eye perspective, it's clear to me that the ease with which children learn to read is influenced by a variety of factors, including those related to past lives. A child whose most recent previous incarnations were in the United States or England would likely be able to learn to read English more quickly than one who had previously lived in a country where another language was dominant. Judging a person's abilities with a superficial level of perception and holding to that judgment is a destructive use of focus.

When my son was in middle school, I saw that, in general, he was underachieving, so I hired a graduate student to help him along. One day I asked his tutor how he was doing, to which she replied, "Well, he'll never be a scholar." My response was, "That is *exactly* what he will be." It was obvious that she was judging my son and his potential by his performance as a twelve-year-old boy; regrettably, her attitude was affecting his progress. Fortunately, I was able to see his potential. I also had the knowledge that he'd been a scholar in many previous incarnations. I wasn't at all surprised when he eventually mastered not only Mandarin and classical Chinese but also the nuances of Chinese philosophy necessary for his translations of ancient texts.

The ability to hold a focus can be used in an infinite number of ways, sometimes empowering people whose motives or understanding are less than ideal. For instance, I once counseled a woman who decided to move to California to follow a guru. I hadn't heard of him before, and, curious, I attended a gathering to observe him while he taught. When I entered the meeting room, I was pleased to clairvoyantly see it filled with light—a clear sign of positive attitudes. But a little while later, as the guru walked over to the armchair in front of the audience, I was startled to observe his gray aura, a color indicating confusion. I asked one of my guides, "How can the room be filled with such light and the aura of the teacher be so gray?"

My guide responded that when people collectively focus on something or someone, a powerful feeling of unity is created. He went on to explain that, reveling in that positive experience of connection, people can fail to discern whether the object of their attention is appropriate or worthy. As we've seen many times throughout history—and often enough in today's world—any religious teacher, political leader, or influential person can engender strong feelings of unity when he or she becomes the focus of a devoted group, even if the ideas he or she presents are misguided or confused.

A SKILL THAT CAN BE PRACTICED

Holding focus is a skill, and there are many reasons we might be motivated to develop it. In my own case, when I began working with my guides, they made it clear that I needed to protect myself from my own negative thoughts. They stressed that awareness and discipline are necessary to inhibit the tendency to become a victim of one's own thoughts. In fact, whether we feel terrible or wonderful depends largely on our frame of mind. As an innately sensitive person, I can be readily receptive to people's thoughts and feelings, making the ramifications of not holding a positive attitude problematic. I am cognizant that my sensitivity is both my gift and my problem. I was taught that the way to counteract my susceptibility to becoming overly affected by others was to develop greater mental discipline.

I began by learning to hold a single image or thought in my mind without distraction, an exercise I offer to my students and clients. The basic instruction is simple: Stare at an object with a single distinct color for as long as you need; then, with eyes closed, reproduce the color in your mind. Alternatively, you might study the details of a flower or a pretty china teacup, and then visualize it with your eyes closed. You might also try envisioning the face of a loved one. If you lose your focus, reestablish it. Mentally repeating a single word over and over again without letting other thoughts intrude can also help train your focus skill.

As you gradually increase the amount of time you hold an image or thought, your capacity will improve. When I first started to work at strengthening my focus skills, I didn't have much time to practice, so I integrated my training into daily tasks. I'd practice holding an image in my mind's eye while washing the dishes, exercising, or folding laundry. I even practiced in the shower. Eventually, I found it easier to hold focus for longer and longer periods, until it felt natural.

For some people, the ability to hold focus develops quite easily. My daughter demonstrated a natural facility for manifesting her thoughts and desires at a young age, though the results weren't always what she expected. When she was about ten years old, she became adamant about wanting a rolltop desk. I'm not sure where that notion came from—perhaps from seeing the lovely antique one in our pediatrician's office—but I do remember she went on and on about it. I explained to her that we had many household expenses and a rolltop desk wasn't on the priority list, so she should stop asking for it. My explanation didn't deter her, and she kept on focusing on that desk—quietly. Not long afterward, her grandmother returned from a vacation in Mexico, and without any prior knowledge of my daughter's fixation, brought her back a gift of a *miniature* rolltop desk.

This amusing incident taught all of us that in working with focus, the thought or image we hold needs to be specific. After all, my daughter had wanted a desk for herself, not for her doll!

EXPANDING PERCEPTION

When I realized I had a capacity for clairvoyance and clairaudience, I had to ask myself how I wanted to use these abilities—just as an artist might wonder whether to paint in oils or watercolors, or someone with a musical talent might question whether to study stringed instruments or the piano. I knew I wanted to steer clear of the conventional role of a "psychic fortune-teller." A number of factors influenced the direction I chose, but chief among them was growing up in an academic environment, being raised by a father who was a scientist, and my interest in child development. In high school I'd participated in a two-year child study program, which consisted of working mornings in a nursery school coupled with an afternoon course in child psychology. I remember being particularly impressed by the work of the Swiss child psychologist Jean Piaget, who arrived at many of his conclusions through observing his own children. I resonated with the idea of learning through personal observation rather than through books alone.

After my spiritual awakening, I carried out the role of an observer in many ways like a child psychologist, except that my perceptions had expanded to allow me to access a level of experience that transcended conventional means of gathering knowledge. As I worked on developing my awareness, I became passionate about helping other people expand their own perceptions, so they, too, could access the same kind of experiential knowing. I've seen in my work with clients and students that when perception is limited by conventional ideas and expectations, discerning patterns and forces beneath the surface of situations and events or behind a person's words or behavior is, at best, a challenge. As a result, our reactions to people and events are often distorted, since, according to my guides, perception informs feeling. If we want our feelings to be aligned with what's actually transpiring, they advise, we need to develop deep and accurate perception. Accurate perception, in turn, allows us to choose the wisest and most appropriate response.

For example, if a grocery store cashier isn't particularly friendly, instead of taking it personally or absorbing the negativity, I'll use deep focus to peer beneath the unpleasant attitude or behavior. Sometimes I'll see that the cashier simply isn't feeling physically well. Sometimes I'll detect emotional turmoil related to a divorce, or resentment over feeling trapped in their job. The underlying causes vary from person to person, situation to situation. As my guides say, "Everyone has a story." In every case, I try to remember that when people behave in ways that are abrasive, sullen, or otherwise disagreeable, their conduct is a direct reflection of the gap between their beautiful Spirit and their conscious state of awareness in that moment. When I take the time to look deeply and recognize this gap, I'm naturally moved to compassion.

Of course, many people aren't even aware of the root causes of their feelings, attitudes, and behaviors. My guides say that people experience life through the lens of their own issues. Someone struggling with low self-esteem, for instance, is liable to interpret even the most constructive criticism as blame or judgment. When we work at deepening and expanding perception, we gradually become more conscious of our own patterns and motivations. I worked with a client who consistently blamed other people—her former husband, parents, and siblings—for the problems in her life. When she was finally able to assess her situation clearly through her third eye, she discovered that fixating on others was a strategy she'd unconsciously devised in order to avoid looking at her own weaknesses.

Shifting perspective, as my client did, is challenging, because it requires stepping outside a deeply ingrained habit of avoiding issues that make us uncomfortable. Ignorance is bliss, as the old saying goes. Enlightenment—the wisdom and clarity that comes from actualizing our spiritual nature with consistency—is bliss of an entirely different order, according to my guides: a serene, unwavering recognition of the justice, order, and purpose underlying all things. Most people remain stuck in the middle ground between complete ignorance and enlightenment, while evading questions that might threaten a fragile, familiar complacency.

Yet the immense practical value of cultivating a broader, clearer, and more compassionate point of view cannot be understated. As our perspective expands, so does our sense of identity and purpose. Fear and bias begin to dissipate when we see and feel ourselves as Spirit temporarily on the earth, allowing us to look more honestly at our situations and ourselves and ask, "Given what is and who I am, what should I do?" Instead of being overwhelmed by the apparent injustice in our own lives and in the world, we begin to recognize a profound and meaningful order, a framework that enables us to navigate the complexity of life more easily and respond to situations in appropriate and spiritually attuned ways. At the same time, a deep sense of curiosity arises. As we look at ourselves, others, events, and situations, we begin to wonder, *What is this about? Why is this happening? What can I learn?*

So how do we begin developing this expanded view?

PROJECTING CONSCIOUSNESS: TRAINING IN EXPANSION

Consciousness isn't confined to the physical body. My guides have taught me that I can project my consciousness as a kind of remote-viewing tool for gathering knowledge and practical information. In fact, a significant part of my counseling work involves projecting my consciousness in order to "read" people and situations. For example, I once had a client who began an extramarital affair with a man she'd only recently met. I listened objectively as she enthusiastically described his wonderful qualities, their special bond, and the strength of their love, as well as her plan for gradually ending her marriage so she and her lover could be together. When she was finished, I asked for the man's name and projected my consciousness into him. Immediately, I saw his energy in my mind's eye, swirling and convoluted; at the same time, I was certain that he was neither honest nor committed to the relationship with my client.

The information I retrieved from projecting my consciousness guided me to counsel my client in a way that would protect her while allowing her to learn and grow. I gently explained to her that people are usually more complicated than they appear, and initial impressions aren't necessarily reliable indicators of someone's character.

I suggested she proceed slowly and cautiously, because she didn't really know this man yet. I taught her how to use her third eye to examine her feelings and the situation more clearly and objectively. Fortunately for her, she accepted my suggestion, and applying a third eye perspective not only helped her avoid being completely carried away by her romantic passion but also protected her from feeling completely devastated when she eventually discovered her lover in bed with another woman.

Like holding focus, projecting consciousness is a skill that can be learned and developed through practice. One of the simplest ways to begin is to visualize awareness as a fishing line cast into the object of attention. In classes and workshops, I invite my students to imagine pitching their awareness into a person or object, as if they were casting a fishing line into water.

When I teach introductory classes on projecting consciousness, I use color as the first "destination." This is based in part on an unusual clairvoyant experience I had many years ago. For two weeks, I was able to see colored light coming out of people's mouths whenever they spoke. My guides explained that this experience was intended to teach me that the words people use don't always reflect the entirety of a particular situation, and the feelings behind the words are a significant part of any communication. During that period, I learned that every thought, word, and action has an associated color, linked to specific emotions. Someone can say, "I love you," but the color of the emotions might be red with passion, pink with tenderness, or greenish brown with anxiety. One day in the parking lot of our local food market, for example, I noticed a couple arguing intensely with each other. A dark red light flashed back and forth between them. There was no doubt in my mind that the color was an energetic expression of their anger.

Many of us instinctively understand the qualities of colors. We dress active toddlers in strong primary colors, while using gentle pastels for infants. Even our traffic lights reflect color awareness. Intense red signals "stop," healing green beckons "go," and thoughtful yellow suggests "caution." Of course, every color has an infinite number of tints and shades, each with its own very particular qualities; therefore, when I teach classes on color interpretation, I don't provide a list of colors and their attributes. Instead, I teach a technique of projecting consciousness into colors that allows students to feel and experience their qualities directly for themselves, rather than ask them to memorize lists of associations. This approach turns out to be a very handy way of learning how to use deep focus and projecting consciousness to see beneath appearances.

I begin by placing a piece of red fabric in the center of the room and asking students to project their consciousness into it. Most of them experience red as extroverted and intense, but this doesn't mean that everyone feels the same way about these qualities. Some people like the vibrancy of red while others find it unpleasant or intimidating. I also follow my guides' instruction that "subtlety, the language of Spirit, is most easily understood through comparison." So after red, I next put a blue cloth in front of the class, and as people feel the cool, introverted qualities of blue, the contrasting characteristics of red become more apparent. Try this on your own, using comparison to project your consciousness into different colors, training yourself to sense their different qualities and the feeling of your consciousness being stretched outside your body.

An interesting situation occurred in a class I taught some time ago. When I place a piece of colored fabric in the center of the room, I usually don't identify the color, assuming everyone can see it. But in one class, I didn't know that one of the students was color-blind. Later, we learned from this man that his visual experience of the assortment of colors I had displayed was a variety of shades of gray. We also learned that when I put a pale pink cloth in the center of the room, he sensed the very same qualities everyone else did: tenderness, softness, and gentleness. As he told us, he felt the emanation of each color even though he couldn't tell what color it actually was. His explanation was a confirmation that colors have actual qualities, not just cultural interpretations.

As you become more adept at deep focus, you may activate the ability to see auras. In recognizing the characteristics of different colors, you may also become aware that colors of the material world differ from colors in auras and in the spiritual world. Spiritual colors are often more vivid and scintillating and can indicate different qualities from colors that appear in the physical world, but you can still use the same projecting process for interpretation. For instance, if you see a color in someone's aura—one of the first steps in beginning to use deep focus to see beneath appearances—all you need to do is project your awareness into it and examine it with your mind to experience what it represents. Brown is a good example of the difference between spiritual and worldly attributes of color. In the aura, brown can indicate selfishness, while a brown coat can feel grounded and comforting. Wearing clothes in earthy tones—colors that have a little bit of mud thrown in—helps anchor my etheric nature.

Developing the ability to project your consciousness into a color offers at least two important lessons. First, it's a simple way to begin to directly experience that consciousness can be intentionally expanded and directed. My guides say, "Consciousness is like a rubber band that can be stretched in all directions." As a fundamental aspect of Spirit, consciousness is unlimited. It extends beyond the confines of the physical body, so even while we inhabit human form we can be partly in our bodies and partly stretched into other places or people.

One of the first times I remember intentionally projecting my consciousness was while sitting with my friend Emily one rainy afternoon in her home office. Emily had always wanted to travel, but with three children and not much in the way of financial resources, her options were limited. So that afternoon we decided to travel around the world together through photographs in a pile of *National Geographic* magazines. We projected into various beautiful and interesting pictures and enjoyed strikingly vivid experiences, traveling with our minds. I remember hearing the sounds of a bustling city and the sensation of being on a sandy beach—the warmth of the sun on my face, the salt smell of the ocean—as if I were physically there. Eventually Emily got her wish and traveled extensively, but the skill of projecting consciousness kept her from feeling deprived while her children were growing up.

The second lesson offered by learning to project your consciousness is that once you do so, you can develop this skill to gain insight and understanding, to heal, and to enhance the quality of life for yourself and others.

THE NEXT STEP: PROJECTING COLORED LIGHT

My friend Tom Bartlett, a healer from New Zealand, used colored light to heal people with disease. "When a person needs a certain quality to feel well-being," he explained, "the color that contains that quality can heal them."

You can visualize and project colored light to correct a variety of imbalances in yourself and others. To use one example, when my son was young, he woke me up one night with a severe cough. I knew I had to help him so we could both get some sleep. Since we had no cough medicine in the house, I decided that I would have to heal him through visualization. I sat on the floor of his room and meditated while he lay in his bed coughing. I visualized his throat area filled with purple light. In terms of the chakra system, the throat is the center of confidence and power, and since my son was going through a period of self-doubt at the time, I sent him compassionate purple light to help him stop being so hard on himself. While focused so intensely, I lost all track of time, but suddenly I noticed that the room was quiet and the coughing had stopped.

I'd first learned how powerful sending light could be when I was feeling desperate to find a solution to the endless crying of my colicky baby daughter. Necessity really is the mother of invention! One day I decided I couldn't take the crying any longer; I'd simply have to take charge and use my mind to improve the situation. I put my daughter in her crib and, with intense determination, started visualizing golden light falling on her like a gentle rain, to soothe and quiet her. My guides have described golden light as the light of the enlightened individual, for it contains qualities of fundamental spiritual principles such as peace, wisdom, unconditional love, balance, and trust. Because of its nature, golden light is an all-purpose light. Even though I approached this situation with confidence, I was still amazed when my daughter quickly fell asleep. Exhausted, I fell asleep, too, but within a short time my daughter woke up. I needed something more, so I decided to create a thought form of a showerhead over her crib that would continue to sprinkle golden light for a time even after I was asleep. It worked long enough for me to get some rest. Whenever she'd wake up, I'd reestablish the image.

I began to experiment. When I vacuumed my house, I took in the dirt and visualized sending out golden light. My house began to glow and felt warmer and more inviting. After a busy day of stress and strain out in the world, I could come home and be soothed and comforted by my house's reservoir of light. Gradually, I began projecting light as a complement to everything I did. When I cooked, I sprinkled in light along with the salt. When I did laundry, I visualized adding golden light along with the laundry detergent. I sent light to strangers when I walked down the street; and when I read or listened to the national or world news, I responded to painful stories with light. I discovered that I could change my mood and the mood of others by projecting my consciousness and visualizing golden light.

When I teach people how to project light, they're often amazed by the results. A short time ago, a man in my class told the story of sending his estranged mother golden light in his mind every day for about two weeks. Unexpectedly, he received a phone call from his father, who said that his mother wanted to speak with him, something that hadn't happened in years. A positive conversation with his mother ensued, renewing their relationship. He believed the golden light facilitated this breakthrough.

Another person in the same class had a twenty-one-year-old daughter who was living at home and not doing very well; she was consistently unproductive and spent most of her time alone in her room with the door shut. After receiving a steady stream of golden light from her mother, she started keeping her door open, an overture of connection and conversation.

My guides say, "Light creates attitudes and attitudes can create light." When we make dinner we're seasoning our food with our attitudes. If you love the creative process of cooking and feel love for the people you are cooking for, you're actually projecting light that will enhance the taste and health of the food. If you resent cooking another meal and the people who eat it, you're effectively tainting the meal with negative vibrations and dank, dark colors. Everything is energy, and our energy has an impact on our environment and the people we come in contact with.

To test whether projecting light really makes a difference, a friend and I conducted an experiment. We squeezed oranges into juice and put the juice into two glasses. In one glass, I used visualization to sprinkle the juice with golden light. Then my friend's wife, son, and daughter tasted the two samples of juice. All of them thought the juice with the added light tasted better. You can try this experiment at your house to see if the positive attitudes created through visualizing light make your food taste better.

I should mention that some people have been taught to send white instead of gold as a helping light. My guides say that white light is the light of "pure Spirit." When I send the mental image of white light to someone, my ability to understand the complexity of the individual is eclipsed by the feeling of Oneness. However, when I project golden light, I'm able to feel both a person's spiritual qualities and his or her particular state of awareness at the time. As far as I'm concerned, golden light provides a more complete picture. You can compare the difference for yourself. As explained previously, comparison is the best way to learn to read subtle differences, and the same principle holds for projecting different-colored light. In general, I'd say that a variety of colors can be helpful, but I've found that golden light is all-purpose.

HOW FAR CAN YOU PROJECT?

Bearing in mind that my guides had taught me about the elasticity of consciousness, when I was still married to my former husband, we tried an experiment with a friend of ours who had moved to Japan. The three of us decided to see if we could send and receive specific colors of light halfway around the world. We all meditated together at a designated time, taking into account the difference in time zones. During the first meditation, our friend chose a color and visualized it traveling to my former husband and me. Next—since our experiment took place before e-mail became available to the general public—we wrote him a letter, confirming the color he'd sent. During the second meditation, we sent a color with our minds to our friend in Japan, and he wrote back telling us the color he'd received. In both trials, the color sent by projecting consciousness was accurately received.

Not everyone is equally receptive to light. Some people may not feel they deserve to receive it, or they may not want the clarity it offers. When someone resists absorbing golden light, I've found that projecting blue light can be a more effective option. "Spirit blue," as I call it, is the color of the infinite; it creates expansion and can open up a narrow-minded person or soothe someone who is frightened or doesn't feel deserving. Most people feel unthreatened by the color blue, because it's gentle and therefore more easily accepted than the more intense gold. Another option is visualizing just a drop of golden light falling on someone and then gradually increasing the amount over time. Using your own consciousness as a guide, you can adjust the intensity and duration of the projection, depending on the situation. Many of my students think they won't be able to tell whether or not someone will absorb light, but when they're in a meditative state and focused in their third eye most of them can sense whether a person is absorbing or repelling. Projecting light always makes a positive contribution, even when you feel you have no obvious influence over a situation. As my guides say, "No effort is ever wasted."

As mentioned in an earlier chapter, my guides compare consciousness to a light switch on the wall. When we walk into a dark room we can't see the furniture, drapes, and paintings in that room until we turn on the light. All those things were there before we switched on the light, but we couldn't see them. The same principle holds with colored light. It's already everywhere and available, but we can use our consciousness to harness and direct it to where we want it to go. The light doesn't actually come from us. It's experienced because we've "switched it on" by directing and focusing our awareness. If we visualize light solely coming from ourselves, we can become physically or emotionally depleted, but if we recognize that it comes from an infinite source, then as we give, we also receive.

When I teach people some of these exercises they're often so astonished that they can't help but smile, because the feeling of being immersed in golden light is wonderful. Imagine being embraced by the force of spiritual principles. Try it for yourself. Next time you take a shower, close your eyes and envision golden light cleansing your whole being while the water is cleansing your body.

Once you've practiced directing light around yourself, take the process a step further. Begin to think of your consciousness as something that can stretch in all directions. Choose a person and start visualizing sending him or her golden light in the form of gentle rain. In meditation, use deep focus to sense whether that person absorbs or repels the light, and depending on his or her degree of receptivity, make adjustments in the amount and intensity. Observe how the light affects that person over time. Remember, golden light can do no harm. It is essentially love, balance, acceptance, peace, clarity—all qualities that are helpful for everyone.

TUNING IN TO PEOPLE

It's not uncommon for people to project their consciousness without even knowing it. For example, when a stranger enters a roomful of people and everyone turns to see who it is, each person projects consciousness past his or her body to receive impressions of the newcomer. However, when the technique of projecting consciousness is understood and practiced as a skill, it can be used at will to tune in to people for very specific insights at physical, emotional, or spiritual levels.

There are many ways to tune in to people. One approach begins by mentally showering a person with golden light, which functions like a flashlight, illuminating the person or the aspect of the person we want to know about. The positive nature of golden light also protects us from becoming overwhelmed by other people's issues. Use whatever image seems applicable and comfortable: perhaps a watering can that sprinkles golden rain on the recipient, or a wave of light that envelops him or her. Then, knowing that consciousness can stretch to its destination, visualize your consciousness entering the individual. This process works equally well whether the person is beside you or on the other side of the world.

When you use this technique with others, be prepared for three potential responses. The individual may simply absorb the light you project, which indicates that he or she is comfortable receiving the spiritual qualities inherent in the light. A second possibility is that the light you project will be repelled, which is usually a sign that the individual you're focused on is having a hard time emotionally, physically, or spiritually and, as mentioned earlier, may not feel comfortable with or deserving of receiving light. A third potential response is that the light will be projected back toward you in a form of positive reciprocation, indicating that the individual is in harmony with spiritual principles, which makes it natural for him or her to offer you positive energy in return. Any of these responses can vary in intensity.

The insights you receive when you project light into other people and observe deeply can arrive in a variety of forms: images, feelings, words, impressions—even smells. Any of the senses can be deeply activated. The demanding and delicate part lies in discerning the meaning of what you receive. Sometimes the meaning is quite clear; often it's not. So you need to exercise patience and persistence, projecting again and again as you seek clarification. You are, in effect, learning a new language. Learning any language requires focus, concentration, and practice, and the language of subtlety is no exception. As you proceed through this book, you'll be introduced to more tools that can enhance your ability to interpret what you perceive.

Though many people in my classes receive impressions or images, they're not always sure they're accurate. The perceptions can come and go so quickly that students often dismiss them; only after learning through group discussion that other people have received identical or similar impressions do they acknowledge the validity of their own impressions. In this way, feedback from other people practicing the same process hones the skill of interpretation and increases confidence in the technique. Over time, through feedback elicited from others and your own observations, you'll develop the ability to discern the difference between accurate interpretation and impressions clouded by your own habits or judgments.

If you're practicing on your own, you may find that you'll receive an image that you don't know how to interpret. This is quite common when we first begin to tune in and delve beneath the surface. If this occurs, try projecting your awareness into the image, and seek feedback by asking questions: "What does this mean?" "Why am I seeing this now?" "Is this image telling me to take an action?" Then focus in the third eye and listen for the response. Often as you start to articulate your insights verbally or in writing, they will become clearer. Practice and comparing your experiences are keys to learning to interpret what you receive.

With practice, you can consciously decide on the specific aspect of a person you want to examine, such as how a child feels about his or her classroom teacher, or a friend's emotional state. Let your concerns and curiosities guide you. After you set the direction with your mind, let go of thinking and just allow yourself to experience what you receive. This is essentially a meditation exercise. Don't pause to analyze your impressions; it interrupts the process of investigation. My guides' rule about this process is "Experience first, analyze after."

In my beginning class series, I teach two approaches to learning to project into people for the purpose of understanding. One involves focusing on people who are close enough to see; the other, on people at a distance. We begin by projecting light to and "reading" the individuals in the class, a process that helps people become comfortable with the idea that expanded perception reveals both our strengths and weaknesses. When we accept this fact and allow ourselves to be open, we can develop and evolve more readily and without shame. We become united in our human vulnerability as well as in our spiritual grandeur. We are all learning, and if we are open about the process we can help each other.

I love the description in J. M. Barrie's *Peter Pan* of Mrs. Darling slipping into the nursery to "tidy up" her children's minds. I often feel like Mrs. Darling, tidying up my relationships through gaining insight and clarity to help maintain a balanced, positive connection. For instance, one night I couldn't seem to fall asleep, so I projected into myself to see what was going on. I immediately saw the image of the frowning face of a friend. Realizing that I was still disturbed by a difficult phone conversation we'd had earlier that day, I gave her a call and cleared up our misunderstanding. Then I was able to fall asleep.

In the class on tuning in to people from a distance, I write a person's name on a piece of paper, which I place in the middle of the room. The name represents the person. As students visualize and send light to that person, they project their consciousness onto the paper and continuously repeat the name to connect with the person's qualities. The process of tuning in to someone from a distance generally demands deeper concentration than projecting into a person you can see. However, my students who have worked with this exercise do eventually discover for themselves that consciousness is, as my guides say, elastic, and unlimited by conventionally accepted ideas of time, space, or direction.

THE ENDLESS USES OF TUNING IN

Projecting consciousness and reading people is a tool we can use to assist others to come into alignment with Spirit. It's also a very practical skill with virtually endless applications. My students have learned that they can project their consciousness into others for understanding and gathering information in a wide variety of situations. Some of them project into colleagues before a business meeting in order to prepare ahead of time and avoid being thrown by the various perspectives others might bring to the meeting. Others project their awareness into a friend to discern why their relationship is challenging. Some simply check in to see if it's a good time to call a family member.

In my own case, I project my consciousness into people all day. I've gotten into the habit of integrating this skill into every aspect of my life. I project into clients before they arrive for their appointment, to get a sense of how to proceed with the session. If I'm on the phone or speaking with someone face-to-face, I don't just listen to the conversation; I also consciously project into the person to see what he or she is feeling. With some people, I don't need to project very deeply to receive a comprehensive understanding. With others, I discover complexities and inconsistencies in their personalities. Perhaps they're out of touch with themselves, or attempting to hide their true thoughts and feelings for one reason or another, so I tune in more intensely.

The examples are endless: tuning in to lawyers to find out which one is a good match in a divorce case; reading the energy of a financial planner to see if he or she is honest;

tuning in to a teenage girl to tell whether she is doing drugs or why she is being so moody. Spiritual healers project consciousness into the body to gather information about health. It's the same skill applied differently. In the past, I even helped a friend find a compatible nanny for her daughter. She'd given me a list of names from an agency, and I projected into one name at a time to assess the personality traits of each applicant as a way to determine who would best suit the family. I could perceive who was easily angered, who was patient, who was neat or messy . . . on and on. The information came to me partly through images and partly through feelings. Ultimately, I was able to pick a successful match.

CAN WE ALL TUNE IN?

I recently attended a lecture given by a researcher who has studied the phenomenon of remote viewing. He cited an experiment he conducted in which a group of people, without any prior training, had been instructed to project their consciousness to a specific location and then report to him what they saw. Most of the participants weren't very successful. Then the researcher invited experienced clairvoyants to try the same exercise, and the results were remarkably precise. I maintain that if our society as a whole acknowledged remote viewing as a natural ability and supported its development, it would be more commonly attainable. As it stands now, the concept of projecting consciousness and reading people is far removed from what is considered normal and possible. Therefore, the only way to learn it is to try it. I didn't know I had this capability until I started experimenting. Now I've learned through my classes that to a greater or lesser extent, everyone can develop the skill to project consciousness.

In general, projecting our consciousness into another and experiencing his or her perspective helps us to understand why people do what they do and how we can best approach our various relationships with clarity and poise. My students are amazed at how well they can accomplish this, given time and persistence. The best way to develop any skill is to practice. Merely remembering that consciousness is like a rubber band that can be stretched in any direction and accepting this is possible can be enough to get you started. In addition, the more we become aware of our interconnection and the Oneness of everything, the more it makes sense that we can connect and gather knowledge without being limited by time and space.

CHAPTER SIX

Positivity

Positivity is our greatest protection.

Imagine walking into a roomful of enlightened people—emotionally balanced, genuinely compassionate, loving, and wise individuals who want only the best for you and for one another. Wouldn't it be wonderful to be immersed in such a positive environment? Can you picture your smile expanding as you interact with this caring, supportive group?

Now imagine the opposite scenario: walking into a room full of confused, highly competitive people in emotional turmoil. Would you be able to relax? Can you sense your facial muscles tightening, your thoughts becoming judgmental, and your emotions churning?

It's rare to find ourselves in situations at either end of the spectrum. Most of the time, the people we deal with, individually or in groups, present a mixture of positive and negative qualities and motivations. Unfortunately, our current cultural environment seems to be weighted heavily toward fear and confusion, competition and incivility, anger and distrust. And because we're all susceptible to the influence of the thoughts, feelings, and behavior of those around us, we often need to swim against the current of consciousness in order to maintain connection with our inner Spirit and its qualities.

A guide once said, "The thoughts of those you know and those you do not know affect your attitudes and your choices. It is important to strengthen and expand your vibration to repel the negativity that is all about you." In order for us to protect ourselves from absorbing and then becoming overly influenced by the fear, cynicism, and confusion we encounter, he explained, we must cultivate positivity. Doing so involves more than what I call "candy coating"—for example, saying we're doing great when we don't actually feel it, or intellectually agreeing that we need to learn and let our feelings evolve while idling along without applying genuinely disciplined effort. Nor is it sufficient to respond to challenges or problems by avoiding them or deciding we're just not going to let them bother us. At best, that is merely a neutral stance, and as my guides say, "Neutral is not enough."

The wisdom behind this observation has been made clear to me through my own experiences regarding the impact of positive and negative attitudes. For instance, near my home there are two retail hardware outlets that are part of the same chain; one is in Somerville and one is at the South Bay Center. The difference in atmosphere between the two outlets is apparent as soon as I walk in the door. The people who work at the South Bay store are surprisingly kind and cheerful, in addition to being consistently helpful. There always seems to be someone available to answer questions and provide practical guidance. It's not uncommon to see smiles on the faces of employees and patrons, as they engage in warm, pleasant conversations.

To offer just a simple example, one day my companion mentioned the streak of rainy weather moving across our area to the woman who was helping him find insulating foam for our windows and doors. Instead of complaining, she praised the rain in a lilting voice, noting that she'd just planted eggplants in her garden. Such signs of positivity are commonplace and I often leave with a warm inner glow and a smile—evidence for me that positivity breeds more positivity.

My experience in the other outlet is quite different. The employees often appear to resent working there and serving customers. It can be hard to find help when it's needed and I sometimes leave there feeling annoyed and depleted. Visiting this outlet is a potent reminder of my guides' emphasis on learning how to resist succumbing to a negative atmosphere and instead to seek ways to foster positivity—which not only improves the quality of our own lives but also offers us an opportunity to become a positive influence for those around us.

Cultivating positivity means practicing a perspective that recognizes that while we all share in the power and potential of Spirit, we must simultaneously navigate the challenges of the complexities of our human condition. It involves making a conscious effort to awaken, develop, and integrate spiritual principles—such as wisdom, acceptance, curiosity, creativity, love, and truth—into the daily aspects of our lives. My guides have repeated many times that positivity also includes acknowledging the truth of a situation, even if it doesn't "wear a pretty face." This is an important point, for too often we can become afraid of addressing difficult issues honestly for fear of sounding negative. My guides have taught me, for example, that being loving toward someone includes both complimenting and criticizing, in order to encourage and appreciate strengths as well as to point out weaknesses with the pure intention of supporting growth and development. An effective parent or teacher, they say, must do both.

Over the years my guides have shown me a number of approaches to nurture and sustain a positive attitude. Three of the most accessible are inspiration, affirmation, and newness.

INSPIRATION

I witnessed a dramatic demonstration of the power of inspiration some years ago, when I was invited to watch the filming of an educational video. As the principal speaker began his talk, I couldn't help but notice the studio audience growing restless; I was beginning to feel a bit fidgety myself. The speaker's tone and presentation seemed overly rehearsed and boring. Then, whether intentionally, as part of his planned remarks, or spontaneously, sensing he'd lost his listeners' attention, he began relating a deeply personal account of a struggle he'd experienced and his eventual triumph over adversity. The details of his story aren't mine to tell, but as he began to describe what he'd gone through, I witnessed a remarkable transformation in the audience. A hush fell over the studio, and people's expressions shifted from restive boredom to active concentration; some members of the audience even began to cry. At the end of the shoot, people not only praised the speaker but also eagerly participated in a discussion of the ideas central to his lecture. This event confirmed for me that inspiration can be used as an immensely powerful tool to move and unite people as well as to open minds to receive and appreciate new ideas.

Many people tend to think of inspiration as something that happens of its own accord. How often have we heard someone say they were "struck" by inspiration or that it suddenly "came" to them? For that matter, how often have we expressed the same sentiment?

Certainly, inspiration can arrive unbidden and unexpected, but we don't have to wait for it. Inspiration is always available and can be fostered anytime and anywhere. Our lives are colored as much by the accumulation of small, sometimes scarcely noticeable details as by events that mark obvious turning points. By consciously choosing to focus on what inspires us, we begin to sense our ability to significantly influence our inner life, even in the midst of difficulties.

In fact, if we look at the history of the word itself, we find that *inspiration* originally derived from a Latin verb meaning "to breathe in." As the term evolved over time, it has taken on different shades of meaning until it's now commonly understood to indicate an enlivening or uplifting experience, or a type of revelation. When we consider the history of the word, we begin to understand that we can reach for inspiration as simply and naturally as breathing.

For example, a number of years ago I was driving to meet friends for dinner at a restaurant some distance from my home. I was already running a little late, and as this was before the advent of cell phones, I didn't have a way to reach my friends. I wasn't terribly concerned until I heard the dreaded *clunk, clunk, clunk* of a flat tire. At that point, I admit, I became anxious and irritated. But when I got out of my car to change the tire, I glanced up at the evening sky. The magnificent interplay of twilight colors was so strikingly beautiful that my worry and frustration just melted away. By focusing on the sky and drawing on its uplifting quality, I was able to manage changing the tire calmly and efficiently, and as I surrendered completely to the feeling of inspiration that swept through me, I also realized that in the great scheme of life, being late and having a flat tire were no big deal. In fact, when I finally met up with my friends, we not only had a lovely dinner, but when I shared with them the story of my adventure on the road, I could sense some of the power of inspiration passing on to them, as well.

The wellspring of inspiration is infinite, and often quite personal. What inspires one person won't necessarily inspire someone else. Some people are inspired by different aspects of nature; others, by particular kinds of music—classical, jazz, country, rock, folk, or hymns. Some draw inspiration from cooking or conversation; others, from the exuberance of children or animals at play. Flying airplanes inspires one person I know.

Most of you have probably developed a private catalog of people, places, things, and ideas that bring you inspiration, but if the most basic daily experiences are considered more deeply, you'll discover an even larger pool of sources. For example, if we take time to look at the food on our dinner plate and really think about all the factors involved in bringing that food to us—the seeds that were planted to grow vegetables, fruits, or beans; the combination of sun, water, nutrients in the soil, and the miraculous energy that sustains the growth process; the life force of a cow or a chicken; the time and effort of farmers, suppliers, and the people who manage and work in markets and stores—feelings of inspiration fill us.

Take a few moments now to write a list of things that inspire you, and keep it in a place that's easily accessible. Then, in moments of turmoil or distress, turn your attention to one or another of the resources on your list and let whatever you've chosen help to enliven and refresh you. Personally, I've found that it's impossible to feel inspired and discouraged or anxious at the same time. And what's really great is that inspiration isn't difficult to access; it's just a thought away.

If inspiration is always available, why don't more people live inspired lives? It seems all too easy to grow discouraged by personal situations or the troubling conditions in the world around us. I've known some people who, worn down by successive waves of frustration and disappointment, lost the capacity for inspiration altogether. But even these "driftwood people" can learn to rekindle inspiration as an antidote to despair by choosing to focus on an inspiring thought or image as a "priority response" when dark moods overwhelm them. With time and attention, they gradually discover that negative attitudes that once seemed unshakable really can change. It becomes possible to take actions—such as going for a walk or listening to a piece of music—that can move the process of transformation along. Eventually, recognition dawns that past experience isn't a binding force, and that a change of focus can be effective for developing a richer, more fulfilling approach to life.

Consciously choosing inspiration as a support in daily life was invaluable during the years I was a single mother. Sometimes I'd light a fire in the fireplace for rejuvenation after a long day, or put fresh cut flowers on our table to inspire and enliven dinner conversation. I'd also play music while cleaning and while driving my children around to various activities.

I've also seen how effectively inspiration can improve the lives of people dealing with extreme challenges. A friend who recently passed into the spiritual realm spent much of his life in a wheelchair as he contended with multiple sclerosis. One day during breakfast he said to me, "I can't do as much as I used to, so now I need to do everything deeper." Then he took a bite of the toast with marmalade his assistant had brought up to his mouth, and after chewing it with vigor and intent, he exclaimed, "Wow, how wonderfully delicious!" My friend exercised his "positivity muscle" by concentrating in that moment on what brought him appreciation and enjoyment.

Although inspiration is a powerful tool, a few words of caution are necessary. Inspiration can be misused as a form of avoidance. One of my clients is a woman who draws inspiration from the beauty of material objects—great works of art, handsomely crafted articles of clothing, and jewelry. She spends a good deal of time in galleries and boutiques, or just window-shopping—activities that lift her spirits. While part of her pursuit of beautiful things is linked to her spiritual nature, it has been taken to excess, driven by a desire to escape the unhappiness she feels in her marriage. Her extreme focus on beautiful material things offers distraction from issues that remain unresolved. Another client, a corporate executive, is energized by the knowledge that he's financially successful and a good provider for his family. Yet he turns a blind eye to the fact that the kind of work his company is engaged in is harmful to the environment, and that the generous salary he earns is only possible because employees in the lower ranks are barely scraping by on minimum wage.

The problem in both cases is that inspiration isn't integrated with other spiritual principles, such as wisdom and compassion, which are essential for nurturing genuine positivity. Although inspiration does produce feelings of joy and exuberance, if it's not coupled with clarity, it can become a kind of "drug" that produces a feeling of expansion, a "high" that can be used to avoid unpleasant truths. Unaddressed problems eventually fester, rising to the surface in ways that can diminish whatever relief or exhilaration inspiration may offer.

Clarity is especially crucial when we use inspiration to deal with difficult situations and decisions. The first step is to shift attention away from your concerns long enough to reach out to one of the sources of inspiration from your list or something new that has inspired you. Allow a few moments for inspiration to fill your mind, counteracting any fear or anxiety you may be feeling. Then, from this state of expansiveness, draw your focus up to the third eye, which will enable you to see the situation from a wise perspective. When you join third eye focus with the uplift of inspiration, situations will become clearer, and insights will present themselves—even if the solution is just the next step in a longer process.

A final note about inspiration is a reminder that it is a key to opening the crown chakra, which is the bridge between the material and the spiritual dimensions and is therefore an important prerequisite for a deep and meaningful meditation. Attempting to meditate without first opening this chakra may produce a comfortable sense of relaxation, but you most likely won't receive direct spiritual experience. Inspiration is a simple and effective way to feel the connection between the spiritual and human worlds, both in reflection and in daily living.

AFFIRMATION

Like inspiration, affirmation is an accessible yet profound tool for assimilating spiritual awareness into daily life. In my classes, I introduce my students to the practical power of affirmation through a muscle-testing exercise that demonstrates the extreme influence our thoughts have on our bodies. I invite four people to form a line at the front of the class—one behind another, like the cars of a train—and instruct three of them to put their right hand on the shoulder of the person in front of them. I then ask the person at the head of the line to hold his or her arm out straight as I test its muscle strength by pushing down on it while he or she resists my pressure. In this first part of the exercise, the person's arm is constantly strong, and doesn't give way to the force I apply.

Then I approach the person at the back of the line and whisper a negative statement, after which I return to the person at the head of the line and retest his or her arm, which now becomes noticeably weaker. Next, I return to the back of the line and whisper something kind and loving; this time, when I test the arm of the person in the front, it's strong once again.

In the next phase of the demonstration, I instruct the two people in the middle of the line to internally repeat affirmative statements—such as "I am good," "I am affectionate," or "I am Spirit"—while I ask the person at the front to stay neutral. Then I once again whisper a negative thought in the ear of the person at the back; this time, however, when I test the person in the front of the line, his or her arm stays strong, resisting whatever pressure I apply: The positivity created by the two people in the middle of the line breaks the chain of negativity. I've conducted this exercise hundreds of times, and the results are always identical, indicating that if we're not anchored in a positive attitude we become susceptible to being sapped of our energy by the thoughts and feelings of the people around us.

Most of us have experienced this in daily life, whether we are aware of it or not. We might be standing in line in a bank or grocery store, minding our own business, but if someone behind or beside us is depressed or angry, then for no identifiable reason, we may find ourselves walking out the door in a dark or troubled mood, or perhaps feeling tired, and not know why. However, we can protect ourselves from negativity by sustaining a positive attitude, and using affirmations can help.

We can begin to appreciate the power of affirmation by considering the standard dictionary definition of the term as a statement that is accepted *as true*. When we accept an idea as true, it lodges in our minds—consciously at first, and then gradually settling more deeply until it becomes a part of the way we perceive and experience the world around us, as well as ourselves. In effect, affirmation is a type of conditioning, a process through which our attitudes are shaped and trained. And because attitudes are composed of both thoughts and feelings, they exert a powerful influence on every aspect of our lives.

Attitudes may be positive or negative. Positive attitudes are based on spiritual principles, while negative attitudes are not. As you might expect, negative attitudes include thoughts and feelings such as hate, confusion, passivity, greed, and shame. Repetition reinforces and magnifies the effects of positive or negative attitudes. "Repetition wounds," my guides say, "and repetition heals."

We can sense the truth of this observation by considering the difference between a child being told once that he's stupid versus thousands of times. If a child is given a message over and over again it penetrates deeply and can become entrenched. Similarly, if we internalize a negative attitude, constantly affirming to ourselves, for example, that we're not good enough, the repetition of that thought creates a fixed perspective through which we view ourselves and measure ourselves against others; this, in turn, creates troubling patterns of behavior and relationship. On the other hand, if we repeatedly affirm attitudes based on spiritual principles, gradually our perspective and experience begin to improve.

We can use repetition to our advantage, though, by relying on affirmations as a tool to promote constructive attitudes. Through repetition of positive statements we can help recondition our thinking and antidote the negative conditioning we've received from our families, our culture, and our educational system.

Every day an enormous number of thoughts—conscious and unconscious, constructive and destructive—pass through our minds. For better or worse, each of these thoughts affects our well-being, the quality of our relationships, and our overall environment. I encourage you to try a little experiment to observe for yourself the impact of your own thoughts. Imagine a miniature "you" hovering over your shoulder throughout the day, observing your thoughts and feelings. If this "you" held a balance scale—the kind seen in images of justice—weighing your daily thoughts and feelings, which side of the scale would be heavier: the negative or the positive? The reckoning is a direct reflection of the quality of your day.

"If you could see how powerful your thoughts and attitudes really are," my guides say, "you would be very careful and disciplined with them. They can cause great harm or great healing, just like a knife or fire." We don't need to passively surrender to negative thoughts and feelings. We have a choice. With the aid of affirmative statements, we can take the lead, shaping and directing our attitudes in ways that benefit others and ourselves. I often think of cultivating positivity as a Ping-Pong game. A negative thought is coming at me and I hit it back with a positive and appropriate thought. This technique trains the mind to resist conceding to negative thinking and to stay vigilant, nipping destructive thoughts in the bud before they develop into habits.

When I first started working with my guides, I had a great fear of making mistakes, which caused me to be quite timid in my approach to life. I'd grown up in an achievement-oriented family. As a scientist, my father had little tolerance for errors, and set a high bar for success. His attitude was, "Don't learn to play the violin if you're not going to be a Jascha Heifetz." That sentiment affected me even as a six-year-old. I'd just started taking piano lessons, and during my first recital, the very first note I pressed was wrong. "Well," I thought, "that's the end of my piano career."

To help me resolve my fear as an adult, my guides gave me this affirmation: "Mistakes are good. They are necessary for learning and growing." They advised me to repeat it many times a day. I said it in the shower and when I was driving, walking, and washing the dishes. I must have repeated it thousands of times. Now I feel it, I believe it, and I'm able to live it. I know that mistakes are part of the learning process and that it's natural to not understand something before we understand it. The process of working with that affirmation changed me; it antidoted my deep fear, which in turn freed me to become more extroverted and involved with life.

For an affirmation to be genuinely effective, though, it needs to be specific. The formula I teach to my students and clients begins by engaging the clarity of the third eye in order to discern the attitude change and affirmation that are most appropriate for a given situation. You'll know it's the correct affirmation when you observe whether it transforms the negative thoughts and feelings associated with the particular state of mind or circumstance.

You might want to focus on a specific aspect of your personality that you want to change. For example, if you feel you're not as warm a person as you'd like to be, the affirmation "I am affectionate" can help. As you continually repeat this affirmation, you'll start to sense your reserve receding like ice melting in the sun, and gradually, you'll feel a sense of warmth begin to glow inside you. Or suppose you believe your sensitivity makes you vulnerable. In that case, you might want to affirm that you're both sensitive and strong. Gradually, a sense of emotional strength and assurance will arise, and even a sense of physical vitality is possible. It really is remarkable how simply changing the frame of our minds can have an enormous impact on every aspect of our lives.

COMBINING INSPIRATION AND AFFIRMATION

You can take the reconditioning process even further by coupling affirmation with inspiration—a winning combination. First, draw on inspiration and then, when you begin to feel a sense of expansion, repeat your affirmation aloud or silently in your mind.

Negative attitudes can become entrenched over time, similar to the way a little cut on your hand can fester if left untreated. Combining inspiration and affirmation creates a force of positivity that eventually antidotes these entrenched attitudes, working like a salve that soothes the injured area and starts to heal it.

The extra boost that comes from this combination is especially useful when healing the deep fears and misperceptions that reside in our souls and are carried over many lifetimes. They plague us at the most inconvenient times and seem to grab us: an experience that feels as if we're no longer in control of our thoughts, feelings, and behavior. When we feel the dynamic of being suddenly and overwhelmingly gripped by fear and negative conditioning, we can reach out for inspiration and affirmation.

My guides say that inspiration and affirmation remind us that we are both Spirit and human, helping us to recognize the creative potential and possibilities of our lives while resisting the urge to get caught up in the drama of daily events. Over the years, I've learned to work with several affirmations that are especially useful in this regard. "I am Spirit temporarily on the earth" keeps me from becoming overwhelmed by thoughts about our world's circumstances, or even by simple daily events and experiences such as being stuck in traffic or shopping in a crowded, noisy mall. "I am both sensitive and strong" helps me stay balanced and feel less vulnerable. "Spirit does the work and I am the helper" and "I am fully responsible for my part" keep me from becoming inappropriately concerned with solving everyone's personal problems or meeting all people's needs. Once you begin examining your own attitudes and patterns, you're bound to discover affirmations tailored to your particular circumstances and lessons. The possibilities are endless.

As you continue using affirmation and inspiration, you might want to call again and again on the miniature "you" on your shoulder and pay close attention to your thoughts and feelings throughout the day. Where is your focus? How much of your time is spent in worry? How much of your time is spent in inspiration? As mentioned earlier, it's impossible to be anxious and inspired at the same time. If you observe yourself carefully, you can begin to pinpoint the moments when damaging habits—which often operate in the shadows—take over.

My guides say, "The pause between events is where most people get into trouble." In general, we handle event A, then event B, and so on. But how do you occupy the space between events? What are our thoughts? Where is our focus? Most of us have been conditioned to spend the time between events worrying about the future or fretting over the past. But as we become more practiced in using inspiration and affirmation throughout the day, we'll gradually find it easier to move into the flow that accompanies a genuine shift into positivity.

We do need to exercise some caution when working with affirmation and inspiration. Sometimes the way we seek to inspire ourselves or the affirmation we express is not appropriate—that is, not in tune with what is most needed or suitable for a particular situation. Let's say you're having a hard day at work, so you leave the office and drive to the ocean to seek inspiration. Well, that's most likely going to inspire you, and while you may genuinely desire and deserve some inspiration, you may also need to stay exactly where you are, at work. If this is the case, you may want to choose an alternative source of inspiration. You might focus on an inspiring memory, put on some music (assuming that's an option for you), or take a few minutes to walk outside to be refreshed. When working with inspiration and affirmation, we must always ask, "Is this particular source of inspiration or this specific affirmation appropriate for me at this time?"

Discerning what is applicable and fitting for each circumstance with accuracy and precision is one of the many aspects of attunement. Draw on the clarity and insight achieved through third eye focus while staying open to understanding through meditation. Remember, too, to be patient with yourself as you work with these tools. As mentioned early on, attunement isn't something we achieve all at once and then sail forward. It requires practice and continual adjustment to the situations in our lives as they are right now and as they continue to unfold.

NEWNESS

The essence of life is change. No day really is ever the same as any other. No person is ever the same from day to day. No view of nature is ever exactly the same. This is the point of the famous assertion attributed to the ancient Greek philosopher Heracleitus: "No man ever steps in the same river twice, for it's not the same river and he's not the same man." Although our conditioning and habits may prevent us from recognizing or experiencing this fact, we can train ourselves to focus on the nuances of change that are constantly occurring within us and all around us. In doing so, we can regain as adults the wonder and curiosity we experienced as children, restoring what my guides refer to as "newness."

Newness is a mode of perception as well as an attitude. Through seeing relationships, our circumstances, material things, and ourselves anew, we let go of preconceived notions and see with more objectivity and clarity. We recognize that at any point we begin again, and at any point we continue. There is no end to evolution.

Newness lifts us out of the ordinary, allowing growth, change, and potential to unfold. Many clients have told me that when they meditate on newness, they no longer feel depressed or stuck. Their creativity starts flowing, because no matter what is happening in their lives, they feel the strong current of possibility opening within and around them.

Nurturing an attitude of newness also supports the growth of others. When we hold on to fixed images of people, we're reinforcing, on an energetic level, patterns that keep them stuck in their imbalances. My guides say that everyone will eventually succeed in actualizing their spiritual nature, but when we maintain old, limiting attitudes about people, we don't support this attainment. This principle applies to all relationships and is particularly important with regard to children. As a guide once said, "The greatest mistake that parents make is to lose sight of their child's potential." When my daughter was struggling to learn to read, I often got caught up in worrying over her progress. However, during this period, I was guided to replace my concern with the image of my daughter engrossed in the pleasure of reading a book.

When we're afraid, we tend to hold negative images, which is the opposite of support. Newness clears away the habit of negativity, enabling us to look at others, the world around us, and ourselves with fresh eyes—like using a windshield wiper to clear the fog that can sometimes collect on the outer surface of a car window. When we focus on newness, we become open to seeing the unexpected, which may have been obscured by habits of seeing what we don't like or only what we would most prefer.

Cultivating an attitude of newness is a simple but extremely effective way to break up patterns that no longer serve us—and that perhaps never have. It frees us from seeing life through the lens of our past experiences, enabling us to perceive what is really going on. One of my clients, for example, is a woman who has felt hurt by a number of men in her life: her father, her brother, and her former husband. When she clings to this way of seeing her relationships, she concludes that *all* men are emotionally dangerous to her; however, when she looks at those relationships from the perspective of newness, she's able to see men as individuals, some cruel and others kind.

In my classes I offer two simple exercises, which you can easily try on your own as a way to explore the benefits of newness. Each involves envisioning a familiar aspect of your life as you habitually see and experience it, and then envisioning it from the perspective of newness.

For the first exercise, imagine yourself arriving at your home. You may be driving there, walking from a bus or train stop, or even riding a bicycle. As you approach your home, see it as you normally do. Then imagine approaching it again, this time affirming, "I am filled with newness, and I see my home anew." This exercise may sound too simple to be effective, but it demonstrates that our perception is based on our frame of mind and can change from moment to moment. Take the time to repeat the affirmation until you sense a genuine shift in perspective. Is there a difference in the way you perceive your home normally and how you see it from the attitude of newness?

If you're like many of my students, in the first visualization, you're likely to see problems—details that seem wrong or need to be cleaned or fixed. You may feel worried or annoyed about these particulars. The second time, when you see your home anew, you're likely to see a more complete picture. The specifics needing to be addressed, cleaned, or fixed are all part of a larger whole, which also might encompass pleasure and appreciation. Through the perspective of newness, you'll likely come to see your home with enhanced clarity. You may experience more gratitude, without denying that there is still work to be done. You might realize that it's time to move!

For the second exercise, look at a familiar relationship with someone: a romantic partner, a family member, or a friend. In your mind, review how you typically look at the relationship. Then look at it from the attitude of newness and see if there is a difference. Again, if you're like my students, you'll experience an emotional shift and a change in perspective. My students initially tend to see drawbacks and difficulties when they look at a relationship through the lens of habit, fixating on areas where things aren't going well. Newness broadens their scope, enabling them to see difficulties as challenges that can lead to positive change if they're resolved creatively. Their view often undergoes some adjustment. Someone riddled with shortcomings is seen as a person who holds potential and qualities yet to be discovered. What was closed becomes open. Where once there was only criticism, now there is also appreciation, as well as greater clarity about how to proceed—that is, whether to continue working to solve problems or to let go of the relationship and move on.

You'll discover that a shift in perception also occurs when you look at *yourself* with newness. One student remarked that when she looked at herself as she normally does, she saw the "same ol', same ol'"—a feeling of being "sort of dense, weighted." When she looked at herself while affirming, "I am filled with newness and I see myself anew," she felt "free," as if she "had wings." In fact, a number of my students use terms related to lightness when they describe the difference they experience once they shift from habitual perception to the attitude of newness. As one of my students observed, "When I looked at my 'regular' self, I felt like there were weights on my eyelids and my cheeks." But when he looked at himself through the perspective of newness, the weights disappeared.

It's important to keep in mind that the attitude of newness doesn't necessarily show things in a "better" light, but in a more accurate light. When I recently looked at myself in the mirror in an ordinary way, for example, I felt capable, expanded, and productive—all good things, obviously. But when I affirmed that I was filled with newness, I noticed that I hadn't completely recovered from a recent head cold, so I needed to slow my pace, take care of myself, and accept my limitations. Perceiving from newness clears away our distorted perceptions, whether they cause us to see only our weaknesses or only our unlimited Spirit. The perception of newness offers a more complete picture.

Newness has many down-to-earth, practical applications. For example, I once helped a client organize her stuffed clothes closet. When we took everything out of her closet and spread it all out, she was surprised to discover many duplicate items. She quickly realized not only that she was wasting her money buying clothes she didn't need, but that the motivation behind her behavior was a desire for the feeling of newness. A new outfit can facilitate a temporary experience of newness and the emotional lift that goes with it. But when she looked at her clothes with newness, she was able to sort them, keeping only the articles that were fresh and attractive to her. As I watched, she started putting together a series of new outfits in a burst of creativity—a much more thoughtful and lasting experience of the attitude of newness.

Newness can also enliven a common activity, such as grocery shopping. In my case, I like to read cookbooks to stimulate an attitude of newness and discover creative ideas. Then when I shop, I see different possibilities for preparing familiar dishes, and instead of the usual items, appealing new choices appear to fresh eyes: perhaps Asian spices one night and Italian the next; or snow peas in spring, fresh tomatoes in the heat of summer, and slow cooker vegetables in winter.

Because newness is quite liberating, cultivating this attitude supports us in being courageous and adventuresome. At any time, you might change your career or learn new skills, such as playing an unfamiliar instrument or, like a dear friend of mine, taking up stage acting in your seventies. No matter our age or phase of life, when we embrace newness, we step out of a limited viewpoint into enthusiasm for the continuation of learning and development.

Examining situations from the perspective of newness can also help us to resist the conditioning of consumer culture that holds out the promise of happiness through buying "the latest and greatest." Many people get caught up in a constant search for the emotional high of newness—a new relationship, a new outfit, a new car, a new job, and so on—but reaching for newness in external things frequently results in unwise choices. The clarity gained through cultivating a genuine perspective of newness can protect us from this frustration and unhappiness. It cuts through cultural conditioning and offers accurate insight into whether our development would best be served by a more generous approach toward the situations and people already in our lives or by seeking a new or different circumstance.

If you're in a difficult relationship, for example, and you focus on newness, your expanded awareness may tell you to hang in there because the relationship is changing. In another situation, the message might be that a change in your circumstance is needed. Every situation is different, and the perception of newness can reveal wise choices from which you and everyone else involved can benefit.

It's important to remember, too, that the immediate experience of newness can sometimes mislead us. When we meet someone for the first time, for example, we often feel a rush of enthusiasm about the potential of making a connection with a new friend, partner, or companion. People usually put their best self forward at the beginning of a relationship, but over time, personality weaknesses—sometimes on both sides—reveal themselves, and as time passes, imbalances develop, accompanied by disappointment and frustration. People who were so happy to meet each other at first can grow to hate each other.

Everyone has strengths and weakness. My guides say that clarity protects us from the disappointments that come when we realize someone is not perfect. The attitude of newness dissolves expectations and preconceived notions, making it more likely that we'll see each present moment with greater clarity. That clarity enables us to acknowledge at the outset of a relationship our own strengths and weaknesses and those of the other person, or at least to accept the possibility that weaknesses will emerge. It's not a shock, then, when specific flaws and vulnerabilities are uncovered—as they surely will be, for we're all human and we're all learning.

Ultimately, newness is a powerful tool for advancing our own evolution, as well as benefiting the growth and development of others. As my guides say, "When you affirm newness, you affirm the creative process. It is the process of change. It is the process of evolution. To affirm newness is to step out of the limitation of human conditioning and into the true spiritual identity of the self—participating in the creative human process. This stops the blockages from impeding your growth and that of others, for with the perspective of newness you put life's circumstance into a proper perspective, and that alone creates liberation—liberation from the pressure of ignorance, liberation from fatigue, liberation from judgment. Do not underestimate the power of consciousness to change your experience and the experience of those around you. Newness opens you to power and potential. It is a very simple concept that brings about the revelation of being in the flow of the infinite creative force of life."

CHAPTER SEVEN

Asking and Listening

Everything is conscious and communicating.

Throughout my training and many years of co-teaching with my guides, they have emphasized that Spirit, the essence of all of life, is always conscious and communicating. Along with this assertion has come the message that it's possible to dialogue with Spirit in many forms: with Oneness, the Spirit that pervades all of life; the Spirit within the particular essence of an individual; and with etheric beings such as guides and teachers, who reside in spiritual realms. There are countless practical uses of direct communication on the spiritual level.

For example, when my son was approaching the age for middle school, I had to decide whether to register him in the local secondary public school or the private middle school his older sister attended. I remembered my guides' recommendation to ask and listen to the spiritual essence of my children before making important parenting decisions. Of course, I thought it was a no-brainer. The private school offered smaller classes and a beautiful campus with plenty of amenities, and having both children in the same school would be easier for me. Rationally, the private school option just made sense. But I'd been taught not to assume, and instead to ask and listen.

So I meditated, focusing through my third eye, and projected my consciousness into an image of my son. I stretched my awareness into the core of his being. I knew I'd reached his Spirit when I felt a pervasive and expansive feeling of peace and love. Then I asked, "Which school would serve your highest good, public school or private school?" It didn't take long to hear the resounding reply: "Public school!" I was so surprised, I had to ask again, and again I heard, "Public school!" With a sigh, I resigned myself to implementing this response based on my commitment to spiritual attunement, but I certainly didn't understand it.

At that point, I had no idea why public school was the better choice. I sent my son off to the crowded, noisy junior high, curious to see how the situation would unfold. The feedback from life didn't come quickly. A couple of years passed before the regional junior and senior high schools decided to offer a Chinese language program. My son immediately signed up; all of his favorite books as a young child had been about China. The most striking aspect of this story is that although we lived in a college community with many prep schools, *none* of them offered a Chinese language program at that time. The public school in our area was the first. If my son had attended the same private school as his sister, which my rational mind had considered the better option, he wouldn't have had the opportunity to study Mandarin in high school. His Spirit's wisdom provided him the advantage of setting him on his career path early—he now works in China—and paved the way for success in college.

Sometimes life intervenes on its own, to provide the appropriate direction and opportunities. When my brother applied to colleges, he chose only Ivy League schools—both because he was confident about his scholastic achievements and because he knew my father valued the prestige. He was shocked and dismayed when he received one rejection after another, leaving him with no apparent options. When a neighbor suggested his alma mater, Oberlin College, my brother quickly applied and was accepted. The large music community and conservatory at Oberlin greatly influenced him and contributed to his ultimate decision to become a professional musician, a choice precisely attuned to his spiritual emphasis. In my brother's case, life was listening to his Spirit, even though he was distracted by the opinions of others.

Communicating with the Spirit within your child, your spouse, a partner, or a friend—and of course, with your own Spirit—can provide guidance about how to maintain the relationship in a way that best serves both of you. Once, a guide said to me, "You try so hard to be fair and listen to others. Stop it. Be the one who listens fully to the Spirit." This profound advice makes tremendous practical sense. Why should we be guided by the confusion of others on the level of their personality when their enlightened self is so much wiser?

Of course the capacity to still our brain chatter is a prerequisite to being able to communicate on the level of the

Spirit, a process I refer to as "asking and listening." Holding our minds still, coupled with deep focus, allows this dialogue to begin.

AN UNUSUAL INTRODUCTION

I begin teaching the skill of asking and listening with an unusual exercise. I invite my students to enter meditation and ask for a "substance word" to be given to them: a word of character or quality, such as *harmony*, *patience*, or *compassion*, to offer just three examples. I inform my students that the word they receive will be their guru for a month. This is an introductory approach to asking and listening, a foundation for learning to differentiate between what my guides call the *bing* of accuracy and the thud of falsehood. When an answer is accurate, it "rings" with clarity and truth: a *bing*. When an answer is inaccurate, it sounds dull and contracted instead of expanded: a *thud*.

In this exercise, words arrive in a variety of forms. Some hear an audible word, others receive a word in thought, and still others see a word written across the screen of their minds. I ask people to pay careful attention to whether they're genuinely receiving a substance word or deliberately searching for one. Developing the ability to distinguish between a word that comes from the imagination and one provided by a deeper source of knowledge is central to this exercise. Our imagination is a wonderful resource for creativity, but in asking and listening we want to receive an answer rather than conjure or invent one.

To help you identify the distinction, first try another exercise. Close your eyes and remember what your bedroom looks like. What color is the comforter or blanket? Is there art on the walls? What sort of lighting is used—table lamps or floor lamps? Now redecorate: Rearrange the furniture and change the color scheme. Notice how using your creative imagination is an active process, just like deliberately conjuring up a word, while simply remembering feels quite still— precisely how receiving a substance word should feel.

Once, when I taught the substance word exercise in a class, a woman in the group said she was certain her word would be *patience*, because she needed a lot of it. But when she actually meditated, asked, and listened, she very clearly heard the word *harmony*. She realized that when she said the word *patience* to herself, she was trying to actively cultivate the experience of patience, but couldn't actually feel it. When she focused on the word *harmony*, she felt patient without much effort. The answer she received in silence was more helpful than the word she'd anticipated.

My co-teaching guide, the philosopher whose previous incarnation took place in England during the nineteenth century, has continually emphasized the significant influence of words. He often asks my students to meditate on the meaning of a word before a class begins. He stresses that imprecise definitions lead to confused attitudes, which in turn lead to inappropriate behavior. For example, my guides define *compassion* as a combination of love and understanding, while defining *sympathy* as absorbing and overidentifying with other people's emotions. They advocate compassion over sympathy. Sympathy, they explain, causes us to be pulled into suffering with others, which is ultimately less helpful than the more objective compassion.

The first time I practiced asking and listening for a substance word, my word was *wisdom*. I was guided to listen deeply and "ask wisdom" for insight whenever making a decision. At that time, my life was challenging, as I juggled the details of a divorce, raising two small children, and building my career. I certainly needed wisdom's help. During the month when the word *wisdom* was my teacher, replies to my questions and concerns came in a variety of forms: Impressions, words, and images informed when to start dinner, whether to pick up the ringing phone, to finish reading a bedtime story to my children— even how to manage my finances. No concern was too large or small for me to consult wisdom. I learned to pause, ask, and listen all throughout my day.

I still ask for substance words. Just recently while washing the breakfast dishes, I asked for a substance word to help me during the coming month, and the word that flowed into my consciousness from just above my right shoulder was *serenity*. I asked serenity what it had to teach me. In thought, I heard that the vital points were to pace myself and to make it a priority to maintain inner calm no matter what. I hadn't expected *serenity* to be my word, but upon reflection it was just right. With a very long to-do list each morning, staying calm and pacing myself was precisely what I needed to remember.

Try it for yourself. In meditation, ask for a word of substance. Don't approach this exercise analytically, thinking, "What word is appropriate for me?" Rather, ask for a word to come to you, and listen deeply. It's more effective to have nothing come at first and to practice listening deeply than to deliberately try to think up a word. Set aside preconceived notions. The word that comes will carry qualities that are particularly important for you at the time you ask, and it will be accompanied by the qualities of expansion, clarity, and resonance. Your word might erupt like a volcano; it might simply float into your awareness or appear as if written across your mind's eye. When the word you receive is accurate, it vibrates in harmony with Spirit, like a tuning fork. An attuned word will *bing*; a word that is not attuned will *thud*. Listen deeply and discern the difference between the *bing* of truth and the *thud* of falsehood. If it's the right choice, it will provide the vibration you need for healing and wholeness.

When you receive your word, befriend it; develop a relationship and an ongoing dialogue. You can ask it, "What lesson do you have to teach me?" For a period of time—which might be days or several weeks—the word can serve as a kind of tutor or friend who is always available. Through asking and listening, you can communicate with your word at any time or in any place, about any topic. Simply pause, ask, and listen throughout your day, as you let your word provide guidance, insight, and comfort.

LEAVE YOUR INTELLECT
AT THE DOOR

Asking and listening isn't an analytical or intellectual process; it's an interactive meditation. Meditation stills the mind so listening can occur. Stilling the mind creates an internal environment that enables us to receive the guidance or knowledge we seek. In my classes and in private practice I've found that people who have the most difficulty with this process are those who have vigorously trained their analytical minds. As a result, they typically spend a lot of time thinking rather than experiencing an awareness devoid of brain chatter. Habitual reliance on the analytical capability of the mind is understandable. Most of us have undergone years of formal education that emphasized using reason and logic to solve problems, distinguish between fact and opinion, or generate new ideas. But if we rely on analysis alone we shortchange ourselves, cutting ourselves off from other potential sources of insight and information. Asking and listening offers us the opportunity to bypass preconceptions and access knowledge that transcends whatever data is available through conventional means.

My father often began a scientific research project while lying in bed listening to classical music. He once explained to me that he discovered purely by accident that this activity opened him up to receive his best creative ideas. He felt strongly that thoughts were coming *to* him and not *from* him, but he was unsure of the source. After these sessions he'd go to the library to research how to prove the insights that came to him in a flash.

If we examine history, we can see that many inventions, creative ideas, and insights have arrived through avenues quite distinct from intellectual analysis. The idea behind Nobel Prize–winning scientist Otto Loewi's discovery of the chemical basis for the transmission of nerve impulses came to him in a dream. Likewise, the melody for the Beatles' "Yesterday" came to Paul McCartney in a dream. My musician brother often spoke of the difference between the songs that he consciously worked at writing and the ones that "came through" him.

We also know from everyday experience that people in all walks of life talk about having a "hunch"—a knowing that just seems to come out of nowhere. However, when we use meditation to consciously ask and listen, we don't have to *hope* a knowing will come. We can seek and cultivate it, holding our thoughts at bay while remaining open and receptive to insights, a skill my guides refer to as "deep listening."

LISTENING VS. INTUITION

People commonly use the term *intuition* to describe a deep feeling or knowing that emerges from beyond the boundaries of rational or analytical thought. But my guides have taught me that this term is too broad, for it applies to knowledge or conviction that may come from many different sources. They stress that it's important to identify the actual source of the information we receive in order to determine its accuracy. Serious misunderstandings can occur when we don't take care to perceive subtle but significant distinctions.

For example, one client of mine told me in a private session that she had a strong impression that she should raise a friend's adolescent daughter, concluding that this must be her "intuition" offering a message of spiritual guidance. As we worked together, I asked her to notice, with the help of her third eye, the direction from which the impression came, and then compare the difference between past insights that life had confirmed as accurate and her conclusion about her friend's daughter. After deeper examination, she became aware of her confusion. Rather than receiving a message of spiritual guidance, she was actually picking up on the teenager's wish to get away from her emotionally challenging mother. This clarity also helped my client to see that it wasn't appropriate for her to act as the girl's parent.

Learning the subtle language of Spirit isn't straightforward, which is why I stay away from using the word *truth*. It can be very difficult to know what is true. Instead, I favor the word *conviction*, because convictions aren't fixed, but evolve as awareness grows and deepens. For example, when it came time to put my first house on the market, I meditated and asked for help to determine the appropriate asking price. I very distinctly heard, "Your house will sell for sixty-three." I made the assumption that this meant $63,000 (an amount indicating that this was indeed a long time ago!). Consequently, $63,000 was the number I chose as the listing price. When we received an offer for $60,000, I wouldn't budge. My guide had said sixty-three, so that's what it had to be! The buyer decided to walk away, so finally I said to myself, "Okay, I guess I'll bend to not lose the sale." It ended up that the actual sale price was $60,300 or sixty-three. My guides had taught me two important lessons: It's possible to hear but still not listen, and openness should always be coupled with conviction.

HOW DO WE KNOW
WHEN WE KNOW?

As mentioned earlier, the substance-word exercise serves not only as an introduction to the interactive process of asking and listening while in a meditative state but also, crucially, as an opportunity to begin learning to distinguish between accuracy and inaccuracy: *bings* and *thuds*.

I first started paying attention to this difference in resonance more than forty years ago, when my former husband and I were driving to a dinner party while reminiscing about when we first met. Suddenly, a very distinct thought flashed through my mind: "You're reminiscing because, at this dinner party, you will meet someone from your past." I made a mental note of the thought, curious to see if this would actually occur. No one who fit that description was present when we arrived and, disappointed, I began to doubt the validity of the message. But an hour into our visit, a knock came at the door and in walked a man we had known many years earlier. We spent the rest of the evening talking about our shared past.

It occurred to me that this confirmation was an opportunity to learn. So after returning home I scrutinized my memory of the entire episode to sharpen my ability to identify the qualities associated with accuracy in order to build my skill and confidence in discerning accuracy in the future. I discovered that the message had come to me from over my right shoulder and was accompanied by a warm, expansive feeling.

From that night on, I began to keenly observe similarly unusual episodes. When I'm unsure about certain experiences or messages, I place them on an imaginary shelf, where they stay until verified. Sometimes the information presented in a vision or a spiritual communication remains on my shelf for years before it's confirmed, while other times it may simply be wrong.

Learning to distinguish between accuracy and inaccuracy is key to spiritual attunement. How else will we know when we know? When we begin working with asking and listening, the clarity we seek may not always arrive immediately. In many ways, the process reminds me of wooden Russian nesting dolls: Opening the first reveals a smaller doll inside, and another inside that one, and so on. In a similar way, when asking and listening, we ask a question and receive an answer, which uncovers another question—triggering a progression of questions and answers that can take us deeper and deeper into understanding.

With time and practice, receptivity and discernment become easier. When I listen to conversations now, I can often tell whether the communicator is clear or confused, self-honest or self-deceiving, by the resonance of the vibration of the person's words. For instance, I once worked as a mediator between an attorney and his client. During our meeting, the lawyer's voice exuded confidence and certainty, while his client spoke and replied in a timid voice. Even though the attorney sounded self-assured, I actually agreed with his client. I heard *bings* of clarity in the timid voice, while the lawyer's confident assertions fell flat. Had I been less experienced in the practice of deep listening, I can imagine that the lawyer would have been quite convincing. Cultural bias inclines us to believe that expressing ideas with confidence and assurance is the most successful way to make a point or win an argument—even when those ideas are muddled or simply untrue (a pattern commonly seen among politicians). Deep listening enables us to hear the intentions and discrepancies beneath the presentation and prevents us from being duped.

A good way to hone your ability to distinguish between accuracy and inaccuracy is to pay attention to conversations. Do the words ring with a *bing* or fall flat with a *thud*? An old friend of mine describes the distinction with the phrase "balloons up, or balloons down." When words and thoughts are accurate, they float: balloons up. Inaccuracy sags: balloons down.

My guides also emphasize that we can learn just as much from a mistake as we can from being correct. For example, when the phone rings and we think, "I know who that is," and we're wrong—that's what a thud feels like. But when the phone rings and we think, "I know who that is," and we're right—that's what a bing feels like. Similar situations arise for all of us throughout the course of a day as opportunities to practice listening deeply and, as discussed in a previous chapter, to learn through comparison Spirit's language of subtlety.

WHERE DO THE ANSWERS COME FROM?

When you ask and listen, it's important to determine the source of the information—that is, whether the messages or insights you receive are coming from the Spirit within, spiritual Oneness, your personal guides, or another person's thoughts. When you first begin to practice, this can be a lot to sort out, but when you pay attention, it becomes clear that the energy of information from each source flows in a certain direction and has a different quality.

Knowledge received from the spiritual Oneness feels like it comes from all directions, and it is accompanied by a tremendously expansive sensation of being connected to everything.

For example, when I lived in the country there was a brook across the road from our house. It was a favorite place for me to find stillness; I loved listening to its voice and watching the water trip over stones. One spring day, when the fiddlehead ferns were popping up through dried brown leaves, I was drawn to meditate there. I was distressed by what seemed to be the end of a close friendship and decided to meditate beside the brook and ask for guidance. After silencing my brain chatter, I asked for insight about my situation, directing my question to the Oneness all around me in nature.

It didn't take long to feel immersed in the expansive inter-connection with the brook, the trees, and the sky. I asked the spiritual essence in the brook about this friendship and its future. After a few moments, I received an impression, accompanied by a thought, that I should remain patient. The relationship would circle back, and both my friend and I would bring to it a deeper appreciation and understanding of each other. This answer felt solid and resonated with my inner core. It wasn't detailed in any way—I wasn't pointed toward any action—yet, in time, life confirmed this message. A couple of years later, during a trip to San Francisco, I discovered through a mutual acquaintance that this friend had recently purchased a building one block away from where I was staying. I reached out and our friendship resumed, three thousand miles away from the brook that had instructed me to be patient.

Knowledge from our inner Spirit feels like it comes from deep within our very core. Sometimes it feels like we've entered a well that has no bottom, or a fountain of light that shoots up to reach our conscious mind. Even before my spiritual awakening or any contact with guides, I had an experience of this sort. The first day of my freshman year in college, I looked out my dorm window and saw a group of young men playing football. I pointed to a tall, thin, curly-haired guy with glasses and said to myself, "Him. He'll be my boyfriend." Soon afterward, we bumped into each other just outside our dormitory, while hunting down the pizza deliveryman. We struck up a conversation that went on for hours. Our relationship had begun.

Messages from a Spirit guide feel as though they're coming from a very specific, close location, like someone whispering in your ear. Even if a guide assumes a visual form in the mind's eye or as an external apparition, the experience is characterized by a sense of nearness. For example, one Monday morning during my son's junior year of high school, after one of many long weekends visiting colleges, I was sitting at our kitchen table, waiting for clients to arrive. Tired and a little out of sorts, I surprised myself by blurting out, "Just tell me where he'll go to college, will you?" To my amazement, the response was immediate. My son would attend the very same college that my next client had attended. The reply came from near my head, audibly rather than in thought; not at all like the message that had come from the brook.

It was specific and also indicated an action I needed to take: If I wanted an answer, I had to ask my next client about her alma mater. I was so eager and curious that when she arrived at the door, I greeted her by asking, "Where did you go to college?" She later told me she thought this was a strange welcome—which, of course, it was—but she did respond to the question. As it turned out, her alma mater was a college we'd already visited, which my son had liked. The most remarkable part of the story, though, was that my client knew the dean of admissions and offered to call her, and at the very moment my client called, my son's application was right in front of the dean, on the top of a very large pile of applications. What were the odds? The synchronicity caught the attention of the admissions director, which not only contributed to my son's acceptance but also helped me to understand why the guidance had come as it did. Guides often remind me of small airplanes coasting a thousand feet above the ground: They can see the twists and turns in our path, helping to direct and orchestrate outcomes.

If you're uncertain about the source or clarity of information or insight you receive, try a technique I was taught years ago by a Native American from the spiritual realm. When I was doubtful, he explained, I could ask the spirit of the sky, the spirit of a tree, and the spirit of the brook outside my house, and if the answer or insight was correct, all of these different manifestations of the Oneness would agree. I've found this way of gaining confirmation both comforting and consistently helpful.

But as skillful in listening as we become, as much as we draw on the spiritual sources within and around us, we must always take responsibility for the choices we make. "No matter what you hear, or from what source the information comes," my guides say, "take it into your own Spirit for final confirmation. For this is your life, and we must all take responsibility for our own choices, even when we receive help."

DEEP LISTENING AND OTHER PEOPLE

Discerning other people's thoughts, feelings, and motivations—
and distinguishing them from our own projections—usually
requires a good deal of practice and experience. In my classes,
I use a storytelling exercise to show my students how undercurrents of thoughts and feelings influence our communications. The exercise relies on the use of affirmation to facilitate
a deepening of perception.

I begin by asking my students to choose a partner for the
exercise. One partner then describes a recent event in his or her
life to the other, who simply listens to both the words and the
feelings beneath them. Afterward, I ask them both to discuss
the qualities of the story, the feelings beneath the surface,
and the energy that flowed between them. Next, I ask both
partners to briefly close their eyes while they affirm a number
of times, "I am Spirit; everyone is Spirit." Then, after instructing
them to open their eyes again, I ask the person who told the
story to retell it, while both of them continue to hold the thought
and awareness that everyone is Spirit.

You might think that retelling the story and hearing it again
would be boring, no matter how well organized the second ren-
dition might be. But the result, my students find, is just the opposite. The stories are more interesting and meaningful to both
the speaker and the listener. By repeating the affirmation and
holding it in mind, both partners experience a shift in awareness
and attitude that allows a deeper and more generous appreciation of the details of the story as well as the nuances of underlying thoughts and feelings. In addition, the shared recognition
of each other's spiritual nature clears away many of the biases,

inhibitions, and preconceptions that often get in the way of clear communication.

My students' reactions to the exercise are poignant and uniquely personal. One woman compared listening to the story told the first time to hearing a babysitter you're not familiar with reading a story you're not familiar with. As she explained, "You aren't accustomed to the babysitter's voice and inflections, and you go to bed thinking, 'Well, that wasn't very interesting.' Hearing the story for the second time, from the perspective of shared spiritual identity, was like your grandmother reading something you're really familiar with. You're accustomed to her tones and you really love it, and she kind of envelops you."

Those who tell their stories describe a similar shift in experience. The second time around, they understand the meaning of the event more fully, and their ability to tell their story becomes easier; it flows with greater clarity. As one student remarked, "My initial reaction when you said we had to retell the story was 'Oh no!' My story was rather complicated, with lots of details. I didn't want to tell it again. But the second time, things just kind of came to me differently. I didn't change anything through an intellectual choice. It just came to me."

No less remarkably, even when the roles are reversed and those who listened during the first part of the exercise then tell their own stories, the participants discern a palpable difference between the first and second accounts. The shift in perspective stimulated by the affirmation radically transforms their attitudes and awareness.

What I love about this exercise is the simplicity with which it illuminates the deep connection between attitude, perception, and expression. It also calls attention to the ways in which negative attitudes can frame the inner and outer narratives of our lives. As discussed in chapter two, negative attitudes arise from original imbalances and misperceptions, which my guides describe as first errors. First errors, and the patterns that develop from them, vary from person to person, and in the storytelling exercise, the first time students tell their stories those patterns are consciously or unconsciously revealed. Some stories reflect a fear of being unloved; others, a tendency to blame others for their unhappiness; still others, an unfocused anger or resentment over perceived injustice. During the second telling, heightened spiritual perception shines a light on those fears, imbalances, and misperceptions, bringing them to the forefront of awareness and creating a momentary resolution accompanied by a feeling of wholeness.

I remember that when my guides first started to work with me, I was told, "You express that which is not within you to want to say." From the beginning, they sought to call my attention to ways in which unacknowledged fears, doubts, and other negative patterns hinder clear communication. Over the years, they've shown me again and again that when our minds are focused on spiritual principles, our inner selves and our outer manifestations become synchronized. When we consistently affirm spiritual principles, our attitudes do change, elevating and enhancing our perceptions and our capacity to listen.

DEEP LISTENING IN DAILY LIFE

The storytelling exercise provides a foundation for developing the ability to listen from a spiritual perspective during the ebb and flow of everyday life, and to maintain that outlook across the myriad activities and experiences we encounter throughout each day. My guides say that when we affirm that which is, although it doesn't appear to be so, it will be felt and experienced. Understood in this context, the affirmation "I am Spirit; everyone is Spirit" is really a formula for remembering what we knew deep within the core of our being, before we took our first breath in our present incarnation. As we practice this remembrance, we strengthen ourselves against the countless undercurrents of thoughts and feelings that buffet us. Emotionally, we become steadier, clearer, and more loving in our communications with others. Further, when we affirm and focus on our spiritual identity rather than fixate on our human condition, all aspects of our perspective expand to encompass what my guides call "the infinite view." The experience feels a bit like being in love with someone. No matter where we are, the person we love is always in our minds and hearts. In the same way, Spirit is always with us no matter where we are, no matter what we're doing.

It's no small challenge to maintain an infinite view in the midst of the enormous number of distractions and the rapid pace of modern life. But this is precisely why integrating asking and listening into daily life is so important. When we move too quickly or become sidetracked by details, our experience and interactions can become superficial, strained, and exhausting. Of course, many of the people we encounter as we travel through life probably aren't in any way interested or practiced in a spiritual perspective, but in terms of our own spiritual awareness, it doesn't matter. Spiritual consciousness doesn't depend on a mutual agreement. Taking the time to listen deeply affords us the "breathing room" to identify our priorities and to appreciate each situation with greater insight and clarity. When we're uncertain, troubled, or confused, we can draw on sources of knowledge and insight that can support us and guide our choices.

CHAPTER EIGHT

Fear and Desire

People most fear not having what they most desire.

When I began teaching classes more than thirty years ago, many of the tools and concepts I introduced to my students were already familiar to me. My guides had worked steadily with me to absorb and integrate ideas and practices—such as connecting with the Spirit within and without, third eye perception, asking and listening, and exploring the power of attitudes—as a way to nurture my own spiritual development and help me to get through the challenges I was facing in my own life.

One night, as I got into my Subaru and headed toward the Synthesis Center, the small building in Amherst where I taught at the time, my co-teaching guide announced that the relationship between fear and desire was the topic for that evening's class. This message came as a surprise, because neither he nor any of my other guides had ever previously taught me about this subject. Naturally, I was curious and eager to learn more. However, instead of offering a summary of the topic or any hint about the exercises I'd be asked to teach, as he usually did, he added nothing further. His silence didn't make me anxious, nor did I ask for any explanation; at that point in my training, I'd had enough experience and trust to know that I'd be guided throughout the class. In fact, it's not uncommon for me to feel as if I'm being emptied of all thoughts and feelings a few hours before I teach or give a lecture; then, just before I begin, a positive force of light envelops me, filling me with confidence and a clarity that surpasses my normal daily awareness. From this state, ideas, insights, and words just seem to flow.

When I arrived at the center, I sat on a cushion in front of the thirty or so people who had gathered in the room, and we began, as usual, with an opening meditation. Afterward, I announced the topic we'd be covering . . . and waited. In my mind's eye I could see my guide, in his old-fashioned, nineteenth-century suit, hovering just over my right shoulder. I had no idea what I was going to talk about or what we were going to do, but I still wasn't worried. I was immersed in a light of positivity that dissolved any trace of self-consciousness or uncertainty. As the class proceeded, my guide gave me, via thought, step-by-step instructions for leading my students through the discovery of their deepest fears and desires, gently correcting me when my presentation of his instructions wasn't specific enough or accurate. The concepts, the exercises, the entire lesson unfolded moment by moment, and in that class, I was as much a student as a teacher.

THE DEEPEST FEAR

I was directed, first of all, to instruct everyone to enter meditation and ask, "What is my deepest fear?" At this stage in the class series, my students had had enough practice in meditation and in the process of asking and listening that this instruction didn't present any difficulty for most of them, and the methodical approach indicated by my guide helped mitigate what, under other circumstances, might be an emotionally charged exploration. Entering a meditative state or using third eye focus allows us to view situations or aspects of ourselves objectively, which makes it much easier to examine challenging emotions. In addition, as I've described earlier, the first step in meditation as I teach it involves opening the crown chakra through focusing on some source of inspiration, and as you've learned—and hopefully experienced for yourself—it's impossible to feel afraid or anxious and inspired at the same time.

Following my guide's instructions, I encouraged my students to resist the urge to settle on fears that might immediately rise to the surface. Like the technique of asking for a word of substance, the process involved letting go of preconceived notions and the impulse to force an answer. The aim of the exercise was to uncover the deepest fear, even if that meant reaching down into a sphere of emotion that wasn't ordinarily conscious.

While we listened for an answer, each of us recognized and recalled fears that were, to a greater or lesser degree, already familiar to us. But the fears that come to mind early in the process of listening aren't necessarily the *deepest* fear. For example, one woman believed her deepest fear was flying in airplanes, but as she sat quietly in a meditative state and listened patiently, she discovered an underlying, hidden dread of not having control.

As my guide explained, and I communicated to my students before we began, we know we've arrived at the deepest fear when we simply can't go any deeper—when we feel that *this* fear is the root from which all of our other fears arise. Every time we ask, we receive the same answer. As in the asking and listening technique, when the deepest or root fear is identified, it resonates with a *bing* of clarity and truth.

Almost everyone in that first class was able to receive an answer; for most, the response came through listening rather than through a deliberate effort to produce a response. A few students weren't able to focus deeply enough to cut through immediate or familiar fears, such as losing their jobs or falling ill. One woman, an artist, described a more complicated problem. She concluded that she had *three* root fears: not being secure, not living a creative life, and not being appreciated by others. She couldn't point to any one of them as being deeper or more significant than the other. This sort of confusion, I've learned, almost always stems from overanalyzing rather than genuinely listening. When I tuned in to her and listened on her behalf, I heard that her deepest fear was that she wouldn't be able to actualize her creativity. A kind of circular chain reaction followed from this root fear: If she couldn't express her creativity, she believed she wouldn't be appreciated or valued; if she wasn't valued, she wouldn't feel safe and secure; if she wasn't secure, she wouldn't be able to devote herself to her creative expression. When I explained this to her she visibly relaxed, as if a great knot of tension and anxiety had been unraveled within her.

I was actually quite grateful that a few students weren't initially successful with this exercise. Those who couldn't arrive at their deepest fear provided a kind of baseline for comparison, an opportunity for all of us to practice learning to distinguish between the *bing* that accompanies a genuine identification of a root fear and the *thud* that reveals an inability to listen deeply or to move beyond surface-level fears.

As we went around the room sharing the insights we'd received, we were struck by the variety of root fears that came to light through asking and listening. There was no single, fundamental fear we could point to and say, "Aha, this is common to all human beings." For several people, the root fear was not being good enough; for others, a fear of being annihilated. Some discovered a fear of making a mistake or causing suffering; others discovered a fear of being rejected, blamed, or guilty. A few identified a fear of being unable to actualize a particular skill or talent.

The most significant discovery that emerged from our discussion, however, was that root fears originate from confused attitudes: habits of thinking and feeling that are disconnected from basic spiritual principles. For example, we're afraid of not being loved when we've forgotten that we are infused and surrounded by Spirit, which is always loving. The fear of not being safe arises from not remembering that our fundamental nature as Spirit can never be harmed. Fear, in other words, is forgetting who we are and who others are in an ultimate sense.

ANTIDOTING FEAR

After we'd spent some time discussing what we'd learned about our deepest fears, my guide advised me to instruct the class to enter meditation once again. This time we were to ask, "What is the antidote to my deepest fear?" As with the first exercise, we devoted about ten minutes to the process of asking and listening. Afterward, as we went around the room sharing the insights we'd received from this stage of our investigation, we discovered another consistent pattern: Root fears arise from confused or distorted attitudes, and the antidote requires an attitudinal shift that, applied over time, restores our connection to spiritual reality—the deeper truth about who we are and why we're here.

For example, if someone's deepest fear is not being loved, the antidote involves consciously encouraging thoughts and feelings that correct this attitude. Often, this correction can take the form of repeating an affirmative statement such as "I am Spirit; therefore I am always loved." For someone whose deepest fear is not being safe, affirming, "I am Spirit; therefore I am always safe," can set in motion the beginning of a profound transformation.

When we cultivate and sustain attitudes that are aligned with our spiritual nature, we initiate the healing of our fears and traumas. Using meditation to determine the antidote for our root fear allows us to identify a very specific attitude change.

Similar to choosing a homeopathic remedy, the corrective solution is consistently linked to precisely the same spiritual principle that initially became confused, forgotten, or distorted. For example, if someone's deepest fear is inadequacy, then the remedy might be the affirmation "I am Spirit; therefore I am good." For someone whose deepest fear is guilt or shame, "I am Spirit and human, and mistakes are necessary for learning and growing" would be an appropriate solution.

Very often, antidoting fear—whether a root fear or fears that branch off of it—involves not only doing the internal work associated with an attitude change but also taking steps to move through the fear in daily life. In some cases, such steps include making choices that provide opportunities to work with and wade into situations that trigger fear. When I was in my early twenties, I befriended an older woman named Emily who had struggled for many years with an extreme fear of birds. Rather than going out of her way to avoid birds, she chose to confront her fear head-on by purchasing chickens and building a henhouse in her yard. Day after day, she whittled away at her phobia, doggedly entering the henhouse, feeding her chickens, and gathering eggs. Her approach to healing her fear was exactly my guides' prescription: to walk toward fear in order to move through it.

In my own case, when I first began working with my guides I had a tendency to isolate, in order to protect myself from absorbing other people's emotional states. My way of dealing with my extreme sensitivity was to live on a dead-end dirt road in the woods, working out of a home office. Fortunately, clients found their way to me, while for the most part I stayed quietly protected (or so I thought) in my rural outpost among the trees. However, as I became more proficient in the teachings and practices provided by my guides, they would send me on "field trips" to help me face my fear.

Once, I was guided to go to an international airport and just hang out as a way to practice using my third eye while wandering among crowds of travelers. Sometimes my guides would advise me to take trips into Boston to buy clothes or other items, which forced me to use the tools they'd taught me while among people in various emotional states. These excursions were initially difficult for me, yet they were an important step in my training. I was being taught to walk through fear rather than try to hide from it. My guides emphasized that if we attempt to ignore or avoid fear, it will loom larger, perpetuating the imbalances related to the disconnection from our spiritual nature.

I don't mean to imply that taking active steps to move through fears is a walk in the park. On the contrary, our deep fears are woven through the fabric of our souls, embedded in the identities we've assumed in our present incarnation and the ones we've experienced in previous lives. Healing our fears requires a concerted effort that demands self-honesty, a willingness to examine our weaknesses, and the skills and discipline necessary to connect with spiritual principles. All of these steps are aimed at remembering our spiritual identity, the spiritual identity of others, and the spiritual forces that surround us, and integrating this awareness into day-to-day living. Doing so is a powerful way to resolve, at a fundamental level, patterns and feelings of limitation, frustration, and discontent.

A SURPRISING CONNECTION

After the class spent time discussing what we'd learned about our deepest fears and the antidotes to those fears, my guide instructed me to have everyone go back into meditation. This time, the question to ask was "What is my deepest desire?" As in the case of uncovering the deepest fear, for many people the first responses to come up were predictable: a desire for a new car, for instance, or to be healthy. But as people continued to listen, deeper desires eventually surfaced. One student discovered the desire "to fully be myself"; another, the desire to be creative; another, the desire to be secure; another, the desire to feel powerful.

Afterward, we entered meditation again. This time, we were to ask, "How can I manifest my deepest desire?" As in the previous steps, we listened for the answer.

When the time came to share, we discovered a connection: Invariably, a person's deepest desire and utmost fear were complementary. If someone's deepest fear was not being loved, his or her supreme desire was to be loved. If the root fear was not being safe, the greatest desire was to be secure. In other words, the root issue—being loved or being safe—was expressed both as a negative (a fear) and as a positive (a desire). The root issue was the same. Because of this fundamental connection, we came to see that the attitude change that diminishes our deepest fear is precisely the same attitude change that helps us to actualize our greatest desire. The antidote to fear is the route to manifesting desire.

In hindsight, this made perfect sense. My guides say that attitude precedes manifestation. If we lead with our fear, we inhibit our capacity to manifest our desire. As we diminish our fear, we dissolve the mental and emotional impediments that hamper our ability to actualize our utmost desire. In essence, when we're operating from fear, our thoughts and feelings reflect that condition; consciously or unconsciously we're sustaining a fearful state, which greatly impacts our perception, choices, and opportunities. However, we can deliberately intervene through cultivating changes in attitudes and behavior, and by drawing on our fundamental spiritual identity rather than remaining victims of our own confused perceptions and misguided habits.

I was amazed when I first taught this class—and still am, as I've taught it many times over the years—by the universality of the pattern. Although people's fears and desires vary, the relationship between the two poles of emotion is consistent. Time and time again, I've observed that diminishing root fears allows deep desires to manifest, while maintaining our fears inhibits our capacity to actualize our desires.

One student found that his deepest fear was not being good enough. "I can feel that judgment resonating through all the choices I've made," he told the class, "and all the chances I haven't taken because I'm afraid of screwing up and of being seen as a screw-up." This fear prevented him from experiencing any joy in life; in fact, almost every waking moment was marked by dread. At work he was always second-guessing himself, taking longer than necessary to finish projects because he was so afraid of making a mistake. He had few friends or acquaintances, because he dreaded that if he spent too much time around people, they'd see him as the loser he feared he was.

The antidote he discovered through asking and listening

was to train himself to consciously recall as often as possible his essential identity as Spirit. At first, he was able to experience this identity only during the times he'd set aside for meditation, when he'd repeat the affirmation "I am Spirit; therefore I am good" to still and focus his mind. He later told the class that at those times his fear "just sort of evaporated and rolled away" as the magnificence of Spirit, which everyone shares, suffused his awareness. Gradually, he began to make a conscious effort to affirm the glorious nature of his spiritual identity in the midst of his daily life—particularly when faced with situations that triggered his fear—an exercise that began to shift how he perceived himself.

His deepest desire was to feel ecstasy, "a real joy," as he described it, "in being alive." Reflecting on his insight during class, he acknowledged that he couldn't seek this externally through some sort of magical experience, or in a relationship, or through buying something that might offer temporary satisfaction. "It's really a feeling that has to come from inside," he realized, "a *knowing* that I carry with me everywhere and every day."

When he described his progress near the end of the class series, it wasn't surprising to hear that the antidote he applied to healing his root fear was also the key to actualizing his deepest desire; his situation clearly demonstrated the fundamental connection between fear and desire. What he feared most deeply was the very thing that kept him from experiencing what he most desired. As he put forth the effort, through meditation and affirmation, to align his perception of himself with his nature as Spirit and human, the false image as a "screw-up" that had held him back for so long gradually began to dissolve.

In its place he discovered his genuine goodness and competence, which rippled outward in all areas of his life. He became more confident at work, took more pride in his appearance, and began to relax and enjoy the company of other people. In short, through attunement he experienced the kind of radical transformation that might paradoxically be described as becoming fully himself.

Another student discovered a root fear of being physically and emotionally unsafe. In meditation, she also recognized that she habitually tried to bypass her fear by pleasing everyone all the time, believing that if everyone liked her, no one would hurt her. Consequently, she'd become quite skilled at anticipating others' needs and desires as a protective mechanism. It wasn't surprising that she married a man who, though he provided financial security, nevertheless projected anger and a tendency toward violence. Her fear-based pattern of depending on others for security made it quite hard for her to leave her troubled marriage. She feared that if she followed her own interests and desires, no one would protect her, so for many years she sacrificed her connection to her inner self.

Her deepest desire, she discovered, was to feel secure enough to actualize her fundamentally kind and loving Spirit. In this process, she learned the power of cultivating spiritually attuned attitudes—affirming, "I am Spirit; therefore I am safe," and "I am whole and complete in myself"—as a way to antidote her fears and at the same time help her to actualize her desire. Through consistently examining others and situations through her third eye, she came to see that in the human form, we are all vulnerable, while our deeper spiritual identity is safe. Eventually, she left her marriage and began the process of walking through her fears one day at a time, and she is gradually transforming her fear into compassion toward all people, including herself.

DIGGING DEEPER

One of the most significant lessons I've learned through my own experience and my work with others is that our deepest fear is a reflection of our first error and our deepest desire is a reflection of our spiritual emphasis. Identifying our deepest desires, then, can point the way toward discovering for ourselves the unique individual expression of our spiritual nature. Similarly, if we examine our deepest fear, we can trace its origin to our first error—the misperception that occurs early in our incarnation process that throws us out of alignment with our spiritual nature. The correlation between our deepest desire and our individual emphasis, and between our root fear and first error, isn't always exact, but in most cases it's close enough to provide clues that can guide us toward a deeper understanding of our spiritual emphasis and the original imbalance that has impeded its expression over the course of many lifetimes.

Consider my own case. My spiritual emphasis is gentle wisdom. My initial separation from my Spirit occurred because I reacted with anger and frustration toward people whose behavior I perceived as hurtful, damaging, and disconnected from spiritual principles. More specifically, I saw the far-reaching ramifications of thoughts, words, and actions, and became afraid of the long-term destructive consequences of ignorance.

But my guides stress the importance of taking action rather than getting caught up in reactions. Reactions, they explain, become part of the overall pattern of imbalance, and when our reactions throw us into turmoil our ability to respond from clarity and attunement is disrupted. I've been taught instead to emotionally accept that we all have free will, and that as we evolve and learn we will make mistakes, and sometimes those mistakes cause suffering. My first error was compounded by my fear that through my own ignorance I, too, might make mistakes that would contribute to suffering.

Through meditation, I learned that my original imbalance snowballed over many incarnations, causing me a great deal of turmoil, impeding my clarity and manifesting as behaviors that were not in harmony with my spiritual nature—mostly stemming from frustration and impatience. In working with my guides, I've come to appreciate more deeply that ignorance is an unavoidable part of everyone's evolution, including my own. We can't move toward actualizing our spiritual emphasis without making mistakes and learning from them, even when our learning causes suffering, for suffering sometimes plays a necessary role.

As my guides often remind me, "We cannot know before we know." In the process of working toward healing my error fear, I've had to go more deeply into wisdom, persistently and diligently asking and listening, seeking clarity through my third eye, and scrutinizing my thoughts, feelings, and behavior. A deeper reliance on my spiritual emphasis is the key to resolving my first error. This in itself is an important lesson. The more we manifest and understand our spiritual emphasis, the closer we come to redressing the imbalance caused by our first error.

Some people have been able to identify their first error by tracing back through the arc of their current incarnation and observing a tendency to react in particular ways to a variety of situations. One woman, for example, when asking and listening for her deepest fear, was immediately presented with a memory from a time when she was five years old. She'd been taking a drink from a water fountain in the hallway of her elementary school when an older boy walked by and pushed her face into the fountain. As the memory unfolded, she experienced quite sharply the emotional reaction she'd had at the time. She'd believed that the boy's action was somehow her fault; she must have done something terribly wrong to provoke him to hurt her. A succession of images of similar situations appeared in her mind's eye as she continued listening: being mocked by a clique of teenage girls in high school; being dumped, suddenly and inexplicably, by a summer camp boyfriend; being singled out for criticism by a manager for an error in a team project. When the images finally came to an end, she perceived a common thread winding through them all. Her deepest fear that she would always be rejected was inextricably linked to her first error, which was a belief that there was something fundamentally wrong within her.

Another student followed a similar process as he uncovered his deepest fear of not being loved. Sitting quietly in meditation, he saw how he'd consistently chosen romantic partners who were emotionally unavailable, leaving him feeling unloved—just as he feared he would be. At the same time, he was guided to look at the very high personal standards he'd set for himself in his behavior, quality of life, and creative endeavors. When he didn't meet his own standards, he didn't accept and love himself, and concluded that no one else would love him either. His belief that he was fundamentally unlovable if he didn't maintain the high bar he'd set for himself was his first error, which gave rise to his root fear.

As he continued asking and listening he discovered, as so many others have, that his deepest desire paralleled his root fear. Deeply afraid of not being loved, he realized that his greatest desire was to be loved, and the attitude change needed to heal his fear was the same attitude that would bring about the manifestation of his desire. As he worked with the affirmation "I am Spirit; therefore I am loved," he gradually began to experience a profound shift in his perception of himself. He realized that as Spirit, not only was he loved; he *was* love. Love was his individual spiritual emphasis. He had become blocked from feeling and experiencing the love within himself if it wasn't reciprocated. Recognizing that, he changed his focus from longing to be loved to expressing love toward others.

Uncovering our deepest fear and deepest desire, then, can bring us closer to identifying our first error and our spiritual emphasis, which in turn helps us to answer the questions "Who am I?" and "Why am I here?" Part of the purpose of our incarnation is to diminish our fears and actualize our desires, so that we can resolve our first error and fully express our spiritual nature. When fear and desire aren't investigated, they can manifest as repression, denial, and attachment to goals that may not be aligned with our Spirit's motivation. When we incarnate, we're guided toward an environment and family circumstances that trigger our deepest fears and desires in one form or another so they can be brought to consciousness to be worked on. We all get "set up," so to speak, in order to evolve.

Understood in this light, certain situations in our lives bring our fears to the surface as a means of helping us gradually whittle them away. Sometimes, experiences may arouse fears we thought we'd already dealt with or hadn't noticed before, which may in turn reveal fears at a deeper level. The process is a bit like peeling an onion: Many layers must be removed before we reach the core. Yet with constant application of the appropriate antidote, we surmount our fears and our Spirit does come forward. If you think of Spirit as the sun and fears as clouds, then as the clouds dissipate, your Spirit expresses itself more fully.

EXPLORING ON YOUR OWN

There are several ways to identify your root fear that needs to be resolved and the deep desire that wants to be expressed in order to find fulfillment. The most direct approach is to proceed in the manner my guide presented during the first class on this topic. Still your mind through meditation and ask, "What is my deepest fear?" Even if you've already developed some theories or ideas about your fear, for the purpose of this investigation set these aside for a while. This is an asking and listening process, not an analytical one. Listen, and be open to the answer that arises, which may come in the form of a vision, words, or thoughts.

When you receive an answer and feel you simply can't go any deeper, ask, "What is the antidote to this fear?" Very often, the solution will present itself as a way that encourages you to see yourself from a spiritual perspective. For example, a typical antidote for the fear of inadequacy or the fear of making a mistake is to affirm that in your essence you are good and whole in every way. Positive statements that foster this kind of shift in perspective may appear simplistic, but they are in fact very powerful, and the resulting change in attitude can ripple deeply through your whole life. As my guides say, "A shift in attitude is a pivot away that changes how you see and experience everything."

When you first apply the antidote, you'll very likely feel a temporary dissipation of the fear. Don't be alarmed if it resurfaces; that's to be expected when working with habits that have become entrenched over many lifetimes. Whenever the fear arises, apply the antidote again, and again. As mentioned in the discussion of affirmations, repetition is essential for cultivating new attitudes and experiences. My guides say, "Often, people find a solution to their problem; they just haven't applied it long enough."

Another approach to uncovering your deepest fear is self-observation—paying attention to fear when it arises. Instead of energetically separating yourself from your body or distracting yourself so you don't have to feel fear, make a conscious decision to direct your attention toward it and allow yourself to feel and understand it more completely. Remember that consciousness can be stretched in any direction, so you can extend your consciousness into your fear to learn more about it. Fear usually originates in the solar plexus, the center of emotion, so use your third eye to project your consciousness into that chakra center. You can apply the asking and listening technique as a way to dialogue with the fear and receive deeper insight. Ask, "What is this fear?" or "What triggered this?" Instead of trying to formulate an answer, wait and listen.

Over years of working with people, I've discovered that situations that trigger fear for some people simply don't for others. Through observing your daily life, you will notice specific circumstances or events that trigger fear for you. Use your third eye to examine the situation to understand why it elicits a fear response.

You can use the same tools to uncover your deepest desire. For many people, the most straightforward approach is to go into meditation and ask, "What is my deepest desire?" When you arrive at a desire, as possible responses arise, see if you can go deeper. When you've gone as deep as you can, ask, "How can I manifest this desire?" The answer may come to you as an affirmative statement; if so, continuously repeat it aloud or in your mind, and notice how this shift in perspective makes you feel. When the meditation process is complete, compare what you've learned about your deepest fear to what you've discovered about your deepest desire. Can you discern a connection between them? Can you perceive how the attitude to antidote your fear is linked to the attitude that helps to manifest your desire?

As you move through your life, be attentive to your thoughts and feelings. Are they reflecting your fears or your desires? Affirm the attitudes and actions that support the actualizing of your desires and that diminish your fears. Many people are motivated by their deepest fear rather than the desire that arises from their Spirit. It's not uncommon for someone who is afraid of being inadequate to want to dominate, leveraging power over others as a way to compensate for the fear that haunts him. Someone who is afraid of not being lovable could become manipulative and controlling as a way to attempt to get the love she craves but fears she doesn't deserve. High achievers who are motivated by fear may appear as if they have attained fulfillment, but in the course of my work I've found that to be untrue in so many cases: college professors who are driven by a need for recognition; wealthy businessmen who feel they don't have enough; women who marry for financial security and endure loneliness or abuse. My guides have stressed over and over, "True fulfillment is the actualization of our spiritual nature. Therefore, make your decisions from clarity, not from fear."

CHAPTER NINE

Destiny and Choice

Rejection is the barrier in the road
that keeps you from going down the wrong road.

After a startling incident that occurred on my daughter's tenth birthday, I was moved to examine and understand more deeply the relationship between destiny and free will—or what I've learned to refer to more accurately as "creative choice."

That morning, I'd driven into town with my children to buy supplies for my daughter's birthday party: balloons, ice cream, festive hats, and party favors. I was eager to get home, since my daughter's friends were scheduled to arrive later that afternoon. As we headed back through the town's main street, a guide, poised over my right shoulder, said in a direct voice, "Stop and have lunch at that café." I was reluctant, as we were already running late and I had a lot to do to prepare for the party. But because my guide had communicated by voice rather than through the subtler form of a thought message, I knew this was more of a directive than a suggestion. Although I didn't understand my guide's intention, I stopped. My children and I went into the café, and after we ordered lunch, I went to the restroom to wash up. On the wall beside the sink was a poster describing how to perform the Heimlich maneuver. I studied the poster while washing my hands and then returned to the table. We ate quickly and left.

Later that afternoon, while the children gathered at our dining room table laughing, talking, and eating cake and ice cream, I stood at the kitchen sink cleaning up. Suddenly, from behind, I felt a gentle tap on my shoulder. When I turned around I saw my daughter standing there—turning blue, unable to make a sound or take in air. Because I'd just read the poster on the Heimlich maneuver, I was able to reach around her from behind and, without even pausing to think or panic, properly perform the abdominal thrusts to dislodge the fluid blocking her windpipe. Had I not studied that poster earlier in the day, I know I wouldn't have been able to act so quickly and without a trace of fear.

My guide had ensured that I had the right tool at the right time to save my daughter's life. But as I reflected on this fact later in the evening, a number of questions arose for me. How did my guide know the café would have the Heimlich maneuver poster? How did he know I'd need that information that very afternoon? Was my daughter's mishap destiny or an accident? How could it have been an accident if my guide knew it was going to happen? I began to wonder: How much of our life is destined and how much choice do we actually have? The entire episode precipitated a long period of deep reflection—about my personal past and, philosophically, about life in general—and stimulated many conversations with my guides.

It occurred to me that if life were completely destined, we could all just "go along for the ride." All of our experiences would be predetermined and our only freedom would lie in our emotional responses to events. If, on the other hand, we choose and create our own reality—as a number of spiritually oriented people propose—then we are in complete (if not always conscious) control of the events and experiences in our lives. When I asked my guides for clarity, they explained that each person's life combines elements of destiny and choice. For some, destiny plays a larger role in a given lifetime, a situation I refer to as a "short-leash life." For others, opportunities for creative choice abound in what I refer to as a "long-leash life."

A life defined more substantially by destiny is neither better nor worse than a life brimming with creative choice; each serves a different purpose and emphasizes different lessons. According to my guides, our destiny for a given lifetime is the blueprint for our learning and contribution on earth as we move toward actualizing our spiritual nature. It was determined before we took our first breath and is linked to many different factors. Some people incarnate for a very specific reason, such as developing the personal computer or writing music that will inspire a whole generation; others come to earth to fulfill a more general purpose, such as learning about compassion, creativity, or confidence. Sometimes we incarnate in order to express or develop skills learned in earlier lifetimes or to learn lessons that were previously avoided or ignored. I've also learned through examining the past lives of clients and students that the balance between destiny and choice varies from lifetime to lifetime. Just because destiny plays a large part in one lifetime doesn't mean that it will weigh as heavily in another. We take turns exploring different roles and learning different lessons.

DESTINY: FEEDBACK FROM LIFE

For the most part I have a short-leash life, though certainly not when it comes to interior decorating. I'm used to receiving specific direction in so many areas of my life, but when faced with decisions about furnishing my home, I rarely receive insight or confirmation about any of those details. For a long time, I struggled with anxiety over questions like "Do I want a blue one or a green one?" A friend once joked that I must have had a past life in which I was beheaded for choosing the wrong fabric! It's taken me a while to become comfortable with artistic choice and to learn to enjoy the creative process rather than becoming overwhelmed by the possibilities.

Destiny, on the other hand, is most clearly seen in the feedback we receive from life. In general, this feedback expresses itself in one of two ways: as barriers or rejections, or as inexplicable shifts in circumstance through which a path becomes clear.

In classes and workshops, I often point to examples from my personal history to illustrate how this feedback expresses itself. When it came time for me to apply to college, for instance, I was intent on applying to Hampshire College, which had recently been established in Amherst, the town where I grew up and was currently living. Hampshire had been created as an experiment in alternative education, in association with four other colleges in the area: Amherst College, Smith College, Mount Holyoke College, and the University of Massachusetts, Amherst. Hampshire's emphasis was encouraging students' curiosity and motivation; broad multidisciplinary learning; and close mentoring relationships with teachers. As I was interested in education, and particularly alternative forms of education, I very much wanted to go there.

But my father balked at the expense, insisting that I apply instead only to state universities. One of my brothers was already attending the State University of New York (SUNY) at Stony Brook, on Long Island. I'd enjoyed visiting him there, and based solely on that superficial experience I decided to apply to a number of SUNY institutions. I also applied to Hampshire College, despite my father's objections. My high school grades weren't great, and neither were my SAT scores. But I'd written an application essay that poured out of me in a stream of consciousness right through the typewriter keys onto the paper, and when I met with the Stony Brook admissions director, she told me it was the most moving college essay she'd ever read.

I'd begun to resign myself to attending a state university, when two remarkable events coincided. First, despite my grades and scores, I was accepted by Hampshire College—a real coup, since a very small number of students were admitted, and in 1971 it was an extremely popular choice, so it was one of the hardest schools in the country to get into. At the same time, the board administering SUNY abruptly decided to freeze admissions for all out-of-state students; because of this unique situation, just a few days before I had to give Hampshire College notice as to whether I would accept their offer, my father finally relented. Shortly thereafter, the freeze was over. I was accepted by all the state schools I'd applied to, and to my knowledge SUNY has never again taken any similar action.

Although I spent only one year at Hampshire College, I had many meaningful experiences before deciding to take time away to pursue my deeper interest in spiritual matters. One of the most significant was a friendship I'd developed with another young woman at the school. We lost touch for a time after I left, but fifteen years later while I was visiting San Francisco, our paths crossed unexpectedly at the office of an energy healer, where she was apprenticing. Was this destiny? Coincidence? Soon afterward, we met up again at her parents' home in Massachusetts, where I became reacquainted with her family. Her parents and one of her sisters ended up joining the classes I'd begun teaching in Boston, and eventually I provided spiritual support to the family when my friend's mother became ill and passed into the spiritual world. In fact, shortly after her death, she appeared to me while I was stuck in freeway traffic in Los Angeles, to give me a message from the spiritual world about life: "It's all about love."

In addition, several years later, when my daughter moved to San Francisco to attend graduate school, she stayed in my friend's guesthouse while she settled into an unfamiliar city and got her bearings. So many personal connections emerged from the bond I'd made with this woman. It appears in retrospect that our reintroduction fifteen years later and the events that followed were one significant reason that life had conspired to bring me to Hampshire College.

There have been other occasions when circumstances

didn't initially appear to change in my favor, only to reveal a larger purpose as events unfolded. For example, when I returned from my sojourn in Cuernavaca, it occurred to me that since New York was the place where I'd opened to a spiritual perspective, that's where I should continue my education. Though I had a place to stay, I knew I needed a job. I registered at an employment agency and took a typing test. I didn't exactly pass with flying colors, but the agency sent me for an interview for a job as a secretary at a very large liquor company.

Then the oddest thing happened. The person who interviewed me told me that her boss wanted to interview me. I went to his office and was interviewed, and after a short time, I was told that *his* boss wanted to interview me. As the day progressed and waned into the afternoon, I kept getting moved along up the management chain until at last, near the end of the day, I was brought to the office of the president of the company for an interview. I could hardly believe it: a nineteen-year-old, barely passable typist being interviewed for a job by the president of a huge company in New York City!

As he looked over my application, he mentioned that he'd been the dean of admissions at an Ivy League university. "I see here that you went to Hampshire College," he said. "That's the hardest school in the country to get into. Why do you want this job?"

I told him about my spiritual awakening with my mother and how it had affected me, and he remarked that I reminded him of his daughter. We spent hours talking about the meaning of life, until the whole building was empty. As our conversation drew to a close I asked him, "So what about the job? Can I have the job?"

"Oh yes, no problem," he replied. "You can have the job."

The next day, however, I called the agency and was told that I hadn't gotten the job.

"Wait a minute," I said. "That's impossible! I talked to the president of the company and he told me I could have the job."

The agency representative told me firmly that the job I'd applied for had been given to a relative of someone who worked at the company. After hanging up, I looked back at the extraordinary experience. I'd moved up through each level of management until I sat in the president's office, having a deep and meaningful conversation, but at the end of it all, I hadn't gotten the job. Clearly, I wasn't supposed to be in New York. Whatever the purpose of my life, it wasn't there. As my guides sometimes say, "Rejection is the barrier in the road that keeps you from going down the wrong road."

I returned to Amherst and set about finding work. As I looked through a newspaper, I noticed an advertisement for a position as an aide in a nursing home. Of course, this was long before e-mail or online applications, so I drove to the nursing home, where I was directed to the manager's office. I introduced myself and mentioned that I'd seen the newspaper ad for a nurse's aide and would like to apply for the job.

"Oh," she replied, "that was filled a while ago." (Indeed, when I returned home and looked at the newspaper, I saw that it was two weeks old; I hadn't even noticed the date!)

But I couldn't help but notice a six-inch-high pile of applications on the manager's desk, prompting me to ask, "If that job has been filled, why are you going through these applications?"

"Well," she replied, "there's another position for a nurse's aide special—an aide assigned to a single resident. I was just about to go through this pile of applications to find someone."

I told her I could certainly do that job.

She studied me for a moment and nodded. "Fine, you can have it," she said, as I watched her put the applications away.

So I happened to read an outdated paper, but in doing so managed to be in the right place at the right time. My job was to care for a ninety-two-year-old woman named Narcissa, whose family was wealthy enough to provide a private companion for her. My duties were simple: I read aloud to her, chatted when she was in the mood for conversation, helped her to the washroom, and readied her for naps.

As the days passed, I grew to love Narcissa. A bit of a Southern belle, she'd led a fascinating life, which included a great deal of world travel, and she enjoyed sharing her stories with me as much as I enjoyed listening to her. Her relationship with many of the other staff members was adversarial; they felt she was demanding and she felt they were unresponsive. But because I genuinely cared for her, she returned my attention with great courtesy and affection.

Through meditation, I came to understand that the most important aspect of my job—and the purpose underlying the unusual circumstances under which I'd been hired—was to help Narcissa through her fear of death. We both loved Emily Dickinson's poetry, so I decided to read aloud some of her poems on the topic of death, as a gentle way to broach the subject. We'd often discuss the poems, and during these conversations Narcissa began to admit how frequently she thought about death, and how the idea of dying frightened her. As we grew closer, I asked directly what she thought death was like. She replied that she just didn't know; more than anything else, that uncertainty drove her fear. In my attempt to reassure her, I told her about what I'd learned through my experience with my mother. Death, I explained, was simply another phase of life, and upon leaving her body she wouldn't be alone; guides and helpers would be there for her, enveloping her in love.

Gradually, her trust in me deepened, and she began having significant dreams. One afternoon, she woke from a nap exclaiming, "Ellen! Ellen! Your mother came to me and we had tea!" Over tea, my mother had spoken to her about death and what it was like to make the transition. I asked her if she remembered what my mother looked like in the dream.

"Oh," she replied, "she had curly black hair and blue eyes."

This was true, and since my own coloring doesn't resemble my mother's and I'd never described her appearance to Narcissa, I felt sure that the encounter had been genuine.

Her eyes shining, Narcissa held my hand as she confided, "She told me your religion is the religion of love and light."

This was 1972, and I'd never heard that phrase applied to religion. In fact, I hadn't really considered myself a follower of any particular religion at all. But her description struck me as accurate, and I realized that in my service to Narcissa I was receiving a deeper understanding of my work in the world.

As I reflected on that conversation, I realized I'd been hired as Narcissa's aide on my mother's birthday—an element of synchronicity that further confirmed a deeper purpose underlying our relationship. Not long after that exchange, I was in a car accident, so I wasn't able to return to the nursing home. However, I had a vision of Narcissa as radiantly happy and enveloped in light when she died—on my birthday—confirming for me that I'd fulfilled my mission.

DESTINY'S REACH

Once we begin to acknowledge and appreciate that an order and purpose runs through our life, we start to recognize patterns in our experiences and events that appear to be related but have no obvious causal connection. Swiss psychologist Carl Jung referred to this phenomenon as "synchronicity"—an arrangement of "meaningful coincidences." However, from my perspective and the teachings of my guides, often what looks superficially like a series of coincidences is really a manifestation of a deeper spiritual orchestration.

For example, the arc of destiny that had led me to Narcissa didn't end with her death. Many years later, when my son went to college, a computer selected his roommate. They became close friends, and when my son was invited to a gathering hosted by his roommate's mother, he brought me along. Our hostess introduced me to her best friend—who, it turned out, was Narcissa's granddaughter. The interconnections spanning families and generations affirmed for me a sense of cosmic order at work. Reading a newspaper that was two weeks old got me ahead of a six-inch pile of applications, so I could take care of the woman I was meant to help overcome her fear of death.

Sometimes the call of destiny takes the form of a dramatic intervention. This was the case for me many years ago when, a few years after my divorce, I'd started dating a very nice man. While I was on my morning walk one day, I heard my guide say to me, "You can be with him for two years." After two positive and supportive years together, I chose to remain in the relationship. But soon after I made this decision, I was reading in bed one evening, when suddenly I felt myself being pulled right out of my body into the etheric realm. There, I saw two men; my memory of their appearance is vague, but they looked old and wise, and I trusted them. "You are forgetting why you have come to the earth," they told me; then I was quickly returned to my body. Although they hadn't been specific, I got the message: It was time to let go and get on with my destiny. It became clear over time that my journey was meant to be with someone else.

Destiny can sometimes feel like swimming in a river with a very strong current. It's very difficult—sometimes impossible—to swim against the current. Those of us whose "leash" in this life is short need to develop a willingness to let go of control and cultivate trust in the order and justice underlying life events. We need to focus well and listen deeply to access spiritual attunement, so that rather than becoming confused by superficial goals and desires influenced by cultural norms and previous life habits, we make choices that are clearly aligned with our life's purpose.

THE CHALLENGE OF CHOICE

A long-leash life presents a different set of challenges. When choice prevails, the emphasis shifts toward turning creative ideas into tangible results, taking a more proactive approach toward life, as well as learning to generate opportunities where there is potential.

For example, one of my clients is almost obsessive in her search to discover her destiny. Because of her fear of making mistakes, she gets caught up in overanalyzing the messages and insights she receives through asking and listening—trying to pinpoint exactly the right answer to questions about her career, her relationships, and so on until she can make the correct choice. However, since she has a long-leash life, there is no exactly right answer for many of the situations life presents her. This doesn't mean that some choices aren't better than others, such as having a balanced diet versus consuming food and drink loaded with sugar. In her life she can write or teach, or both; take this job or that job; and live where she chooses. Like many people with long-leash lives, she needs to develop the confidence to make choices without knowing the outcome. Instead she wastes a lot of time looking for guided signs to present themselves. I keep encouraging her to be less hesitant and more proactive and self-determining.

Another client, a woman who started her own business, chose to partner with a man to expand that business to a second location. I suggested indirectly that I didn't think he was a great choice. But my client insisted that he was extremely talented and creative, and a wonderful fit for her business. I ran into her recently, and she told me, ruefully, that the partnership had been a financial disaster. She learned the hard way that creative choice allows the freedom to make poor decisions. The positive takeaway, she stressed, was to attend to details and not just be swept up by inspiration and potential.

THE INTERPLAY OF DESTINY
AND CHOICE

No one's life is completely bound by destiny or entirely open to creative choice. My friend Sue's story offers a dramatic illustration of this point. Sue and I met when we were both nineteen and newly opened to clairvoyance and clairaudience, a development that forged a close bond between us. She had awakened spiritually through a near-death experience precipitated by a drug overdose. While she was out of her body in the spiritual realm, she was told that it wasn't her time to die and that she had to go back. After being returned to her physical form Sue found her wisdom and perceptions had become greatly enhanced; soon afterward, she committed her talents to using diplomacy and nonviolent activism to support human rights. Most notably, Sue was involved in the movement to convince colleges and universities to financially divest themselves of their interests in South Africa. Ultimately, 155 colleges and universities did pull their investments in companies that traded with or had operations in South Africa, significantly contributing to ending apartheid and restoring Nelson Mandela's personal freedom.

Nearly thirty years after Sue's first near-death experience, she had a second one, brought on by a heart attack. This time, she told me, the beings in the spiritual world gave her a choice: She could remain in the etheric realm to continue her evolution there, or return to her body. They showed her images of activities she would engage in if she chose to return to her human form, specifically related to supporting her godson through a legal entanglement that would culminate in his financial security. Motivated by her love for her godson, Sue returned to earth; as predicted, she helped him.

In Sue's first near-death experience, she was given no choice. The second time, she was offered a choice, but the option of returning to her body involved fulfilling a specific purpose. Destiny and choice were unmistakably intertwined.

Of course, we don't have to have a near-death experience in order to discover clues about our destiny or the role of creative choice in our life. The opportunity to discern deep patterns is always right in front of us.

THE SCHOOL OF LIFE

Life on earth is our school. My guides have taught me that every situation offers lessons that lead us further along the path of actualizing our spiritual essence. This in itself is a powerful lesson, for when we approach our experiences from the perspective that each situation represents an opportunity to learn, to grow, and to heal, then everything that occurs—however painful, bleak, puzzling, or unusual—is both meaningful and beneficial. From this expanded point of view, we can discern an order and a purpose behind situations and events—a singular clarity that equips us to respond more skillfully and creatively to whatever life presents us, in ways that foster our own development while simultaneously helping us make a positive contribution to the world around us.

This principle was vividly affirmed for me recently during my morning walk around the Charles River, when a man with prosthetic legs jogged past me. As I watched him I wondered, *Okay, what's his lesson? What's his story?* I projected my consciousness into his soul and into his past lives, wondering if some pattern of cruelty or imbalance in previous incarnations had contributed to his present situation. To my surprise, I saw that in a past life this man had been a soldier who had lost his legs in battle, after which he'd given up his will to live. I don't know how he lost his legs in this life, but here he was on a fine summer morning, fit and smiling as he jogged along the river on prosthetic legs. It was so clear that his lesson was to make the best of an extremely difficult situation, and that in this life he'd seized the opportunity to relive with a different attitude the challenge he'd faced in his past life. It was evident, too, from the expressions of other people walking or jogging along the river, that his courage and the sheer joy he exuded in embracing life inspired everyone around him.

Almost immediately afterward, another man jogged past, and I couldn't help but notice that he had only one arm. I confess, it was a bit surprising: I'd walked along the river for years and had never seen either man, much less encountered two people missing limbs passing in quick succession. Curious, I projected into this second man and saw that in a previous life he, too, had been a soldier who had lost a limb. And just as I'd seen in the first jogger, I perceived in this man the same pattern of learning to approach his challenge differently in his current incarnation—to resist the feeling that he'd lost his identity and embrace the fact that he still had a lot to offer and experience. Tuning in to him, I could see that he wasn't distraught; he was learning to acknowledge limitation and work with it to the best of his ability.

The experience of tuning in to these two men reminded me of something a guide had told me many years earlier: Although we all experience limitations of some kind or another, and although the circumstances of each person's life differ widely, the Spirit within each of us is unlimited. The crucial point is that even with our limitations, we can actualize our potential. Sometimes, circumstances come together to help heal deep fears or other imbalances through a natural progression. But we don't have to wait for our education to proceed. We can take the initiative, using the skills introduced in earlier chapters to look beneath appearances to discern the lessons in our experiences.

LISTENING TO LEARN

The most direct way to discover the lessons life has to teach us is to use the skills of deep focus and asking and listening. Choose a situation in your life you'd like to understand more fully: a specific relationship, perhaps, or why your job application was rejected.

As in seeking a word of substance or investigating fear and desire, begin by entering meditation. Meditation establishes the state of inner calm needed in order to listen deeply, which is particularly important if the circumstance you're delving into is troubling. Once you've achieved stillness, focus through the third eye and ask, "What lesson is there for me in this situation?" Then listen. When you receive an answer, consider how it alters your perception and understanding of the situation. You may also discover that the answer is very different from what you anticipated.

For instance, in class one evening, I participated in an asking and listening exercise along with my students. The instructions were to identify a disturbing childhood memory and then, with the aid of the third eye and deep listening, gain insight into the lessons and meaning surrounding the event. The memory I chose involved an incident that occurred when I was only four years old. I'd been playing outside with one of my brothers when we spotted a pair of toads and decided it would be fun to have them race each other. We each picked one up, my brother drew a line in the dirt, and then we held the toads behind the mark until after we said, "One, two, three, go!" On "Go!" we let the toads free and followed behind them, urging them on by stomping our feet and shouting, "Come on, toad, come on!" In my excitement, I accidentally stepped on my toad's leg and quite literally squashed it. I felt terribly guilty, and hurt all over because of what I'd done to this little creature. I knew that I'd ruined the toad's life, and the remorse I'd felt then was just as vivid as when I recalled it years later.

With the memory of that event fresh in my mind, I asked what my lesson was. The answer I received was that sometimes we cause suffering because we're not aware of the nature or consequences of our actions. That was certainly true in this instance. At four years old, I didn't know that jumping excitedly after a toad might cause injury; afterward, I knew better, and as a result was much more attentive to the way I acted around smaller creatures.

As I continued listening with focus and stillness, I saw how this lesson was tied into the much larger one of resolving my first error fear. I recalled how often my guides reminded me that we don't know before we know. In the course of our development and learning, we all make mistakes, and sometimes painful consequences are unavoidable. Acknowledging and accepting this reality has been, and continues to be, an important part of my evolution.

AN EXPANDED PERSPECTIVE

Because we're all learning, we're all likely to make mistakes, to do or say things that are not attuned to our Spirit's nature. We're equally likely to be on the receiving end when people speak or behave in ways that are tactless, unsuitable, or even vicious. That is an inescapable aspect of the human condition. We get our feet stepped on; people shove ahead of us in the grocery checkout line; friends or coworkers, preoccupied with their own concerns, can be rude or insensitive; our own frustrations or turmoil lead us to behave or speak in ways we later wish we hadn't. And of course there are extreme examples, such as the invasion of a country, or polluting drinking water, or consciously taking advantage of employees. When viewed from a broader, spiritual perspective, the kinds of reactions we might ordinarily feel when others are selfish, unconsciously negative, or destructive—or when we realize we've behaved in thoughtless or self-centered ways—start to dissipate. Instead of anger, blame, helplessness, or guilt, we can respond to such experiences with acceptance, compassion, and a clear path of action.

As my guides repeatedly emphasize, acceptance is neither complacency nor submission; it's not an "easy out," a tactic for avoiding discomfort, unpleasantness, or responsibility. Rather, acceptance is an unbiased recognition of what is, simply because it is. It is a universal spiritual principle that brings us inner calm, cutting through culturally imposed dichotomies of good and bad, right and wrong, and allowing us to look at ourselves, others, and situations with clarity. If someone behaves inappropriately because he doesn't know any better, how can we blame him for his ignorance? If he had known better, he would have behaved differently.

The inner calm and clarity that comes from acceptance allows us to see that people aren't enlightened yet, so they're going to act and speak in ways that aren't aligned with spiritual principles. This expanded perspective is the basis of genuine compassion, which my guides say is a combination of understanding and love. Through understanding, we acknowledge that we are all human and accept that we all make mistakes—often out of ignorance but also out of fear, confusion, turmoil, or other imbalance. Love is the desire for the best for everyone. It's a motive force that seeks opportunities to comfort others, relieve their suffering, help them to move past confusion and turmoil, and actualize the magnificence of Spirit. As we practice acceptance and compassion toward others, we simultaneously need to apply the same approach toward ourselves.

Attaining the clarity that brings us to acceptance and compassion doesn't necessarily work like a magic wand, instantly and completely changing our perspective the very first time we shift into a more expansive mode of awareness. As in working with affirmations, repetition plays an essential role in our learning. We all need to revisit our lessons many, many times before we can attain the ability to sustain a spiritual perspective that may be appropriately called "the infinite view."

LEVELS OF LEARNING

Not all lessons are profound. If you trip down the stairs, the lesson could be "Pay attention to your body," or simply "Focus on the task at hand." If we're cut off in traffic or lose a cherished piece of jewelry, the lesson might simply be "Let it go." One client of mine, after weeks of dealing with an extremely colicky newborn, asked what her lesson was, and the answer she received was simply "Endurance." Over the years, as she faced other challenging situations, she recalled that early lesson and discovered that it was just as valid.

A lesson might be something both matter-of-fact and reassuring, such as "You are guided and in the right place at the right time." That was actually a message I received when I attended a large conference hosted by the Marion Institute and kept running into a client—in the cafeteria line, coming out of the ladies' room, and, without any prior planning or agreement, seated next to me in one of the facility's large auditoriums. After so many "chance" encounters, we decided to set aside some time to talk. This conversation ultimately led to an introduction to a friend of hers, an editor who ended up publishing one of my books.

Some lessons do have far-reaching effects. A man in one of my classes described a harrowing incident in which his house had been struck by lightning. None of his family was hurt, but the roof was damaged and much of their electronic equipment was destroyed. The event and the family's reactions to it—the initial excitement and alarm, the gradual reassurance, followed by a joint search of the house to determine the extent of the damage—all had a sense of adventure about it. When the man asked about the lesson of the experience, he discovered that it was to draw the family together. He explained to the class that for some time, they'd all been so busy that they hadn't spent much time with each other. Instead of dealing only with the physical damage, the man took his cue from the lesson and helped his family work together to replace what needed to be replaced, restoring the connections that made them a family. The lightning strike refocused them all and created a sense of clarification and priority, a perception that spread out into their individual lives and their family life.

Learning from personal experiences can also prepare us to learn from world events or natural disasters that occur thousands of miles away and seemingly have no direct relationship to our own lives. For example, when I meditate on what I need to learn from global environmental or financial challenges, I see that most of the problems stem from the widespread fixation on pursuing purely personal goals and desires, which blinds us to the long-term impact on everyone and everything on the planet. My lesson is to remember the fundamental interconnectedness of life and to act in ways that nourish positive rather than negative expressions of this unavoidable truth.

All of us who share this planet make up a single vast, complex organism; we can't harm one part of that organism without injuring the whole. If we contribute to the suffering in one part of the world we will be made vulnerable in another. Think about how a smoker damages her lungs and the negative impact this has on her overall health. Now apply that principle more widely. Pollution from coal-burning plants in the Ohio Valley brings acid rain to New England and Canada. The lead in toys made in some countries poisons children in others. Through greed, warfare, and blindness toward climate change, nearly one billion people on the planet lack access to adequate food; every three seconds one person dies of starvation—usually a child under the age of five.

Thanks to 24-7 news cycles and social media, we are exposed to more problems than we can possibly solve, which can leave us feeling baffled, discouraged—or worse, numb. By asking and listening for lessons, we can begin to discern how, when, and where to actively apply personal effort or, more discreetly, to send light and positive thoughts, yet always with the awareness that our thoughts, words, and actions have far-reaching impact. When we focus on our learning, we move into empowerment and creative solutions and come to know our particular place in the scheme of the whole, and from this perspective we can experience a feeling of satisfaction and confidence.

LEARNING IN THE MOMENT

As we practice the skill of consciously learning lessons from past experiences or global challenges, we're simultaneously working toward the ability to ask for the lesson in any given moment. Whenever we're troubled by a current experience or a situation, we can ask, "What is the lesson for me in this situation?" And by listening, we can receive the answer. Once we do, we need to act on it, of course, but the beauty of asking in the moment is that the answer can be applied right then and there.

For instance, when I walk through my neighborhood, I frequently pass people asking for money. My approach to these situations is to ask, "What is my lesson? Given what is, what am I to do?" The answer I receive—often in thought form, but sometimes through images or words—varies according to the specific circumstance. Sometimes the lesson is "It's not your job to meet all needs," so I walk on by. At other times, the lesson is "Be generous and share," motivating me to dig my wallet out of my purse, to offer money and comfort.

We may ask and listen for a lesson as many times as we want and as often as we want. This tool is always applicable. Ultimately, asking for the lesson in the moment hones our ability to attune to Spirit.

It can be difficult to ask for the lesson in the moment if a situation involves a crisis or a shock. I faced such an experience years ago when, after changing health insurance plans, I brought my young son to a new pediatrician. After examining him, the doctor informed me that my son had a heart murmur. His former pediatrician had never mentioned it; when I called him to discuss the finding, he told me that he hadn't wanted to alarm me. Many young children, he explained, are found to have a heart murmur. Typically it disappears after a few years without adversely affecting a child's health.

The new pediatrician ordered an X-ray, however, which revealed that my son had a ventricular septal defect—a hole in the heart wall that caused blood to get pumped back to his lungs instead of out to his body, which made his heart work harder. Because fear paralyzed me when I heard the diagnosis, I didn't immediately ask what the lesson was. Within a few days, using meditation, I came back to myself, and when I asked what the lesson was, I learned that my son's diagnosis, and the panic I felt when I heard it, was actually an opportunity to open up to approaches to healing that go beyond cultural ideas about what is possible.

Not long afterward, I had the pleasure of meeting Tom Bartlett, an unusually effective healer from New Zealand. At the age of forty-eight, Tom discovered that he had advanced-stage Hodgkin's lymphoma. In the course of his search for treatment options, he was cured by a woman trained in radionics, a system of diagnosis and treatment that uses a type of energy similar to radio waves to correct imbalances in energy that manifest as illness. Overjoyed and fascinated, Tom began to study this form of healing. I met him when he was in his early sixties, at which point he'd become an extraordinarily skilled radionics practitioner. He was a frequent visitor to my home over a three-year period, and during that time I watched him diagnose and treat many people, performing one miracle after another at my kitchen table—including healing the hole in my son's heart, a transformation confirmed by X-ray.

It's not unusual for emotional shock to disturb our focus and impede our ability to listen, which then triggers a panicky feeling and confusion about where to turn. A woman in one of my classes shared that many years earlier she'd been on a skiing weekend with a man with whom she was very much in love. "One of those live-or-die things," she explained. During their weekend together the man had spent much of one night with another woman. When my student found out, her reaction was to focus on what she could do to save the relationship. The question she kept asking herself was "How can I make this better?"

In a lesson-learning exercise in class, she chose this

incident to see what lesson it had for her. Ironically enough, she saw that part of the lesson was that she needed to ask what the lesson was! Instead, in the moment, she'd been looking only at the external situation and the options available to keep the relationship from ending. It was as if she was not part of the situation. Had she been emotionally free to ask for the lesson in that moment, the asking would have brought her back to herself, to the knowing within her. She would have learned that she could stop to consider her own feelings.

LEARNING OVER TIME

Of course, we can't learn many of the lessons life has to teach us when we're three or four or eight—or perhaps even eighteen. Often, our early experiences establish a kind of lesson plan to be absorbed and understood later on in adulthood. Even then, lessons often aren't learned immediately. That's why a lesson will be repeated over and over again until we do learn it. If we look back at experiences in childhood, adolescence, and adulthood, we'll likely discover a pattern—maybe more than one—to our experiences and learning, repeated in different forms at every stage of our life.

For instance, one of my clients felt ashamed when she didn't do things well, and her way of dealing with this pattern was to withdraw and avoid. She'd say she'd do something at a certain time—such as e-mail me to set up a time to have a conversation—and then wouldn't follow through. When working on a group project, she would procrastinate and not communicate with others involved because she felt ashamed about falling behind. Not only did she not complete her work quickly enough, she also annoyed her coworkers because of her lack of communication.

When she meditated on her behavior and asked for her lesson, she flashed on memories from her childhood and adolescence. Her way of dealing with criticism back then was to go into her room and read to avoid interaction with family members. She discovered that her pattern of avoidance was repetitive. Simultaneously, in her meditation she learned that she could draw on the clarity of her Spirit. She heard that her avoidance compounded problems and made her feel more and more ashamed. As an alternative she could nip the problems in the bud by staying in communication when she was struggling, instead of dodging issues.

My guides always say, "You are so loved; therefore your lessons will appear again and again." I encourage my students, as I've been encouraged, to welcome the repetition. Instead of responding, "Oh, no, not this again!" say, "Oh, yes, I'm so loved that I'm handed this lesson until I learn." It's important to remember that fundamentally our lessons are directly related to healing our soul and actualizing our Spirit.

I sometimes think of our lives as time-release capsules. The timing in which lessons are resolved or brought to our attention differs for each of us. Other times, I think of the learning process as filling a glass with the water of our experiences. Each experience adds a little more water to the glass, but not until the water reaches the top and reiteration has occurred do we understand our lessons. Repetition is how we learn, and when a change in our awareness occurs, we start to see a deeper order and purpose underlying the events in our lives.

To give an example, when my companion and I sold our

house in the country several years ago, we wanted to invest the money in real estate in Boston. We looked at several places with a real estate agent, and each one felt, energetically, like walking into an invisible wall. None of the places we looked at gave me the feeling of expansion and openness, like the *whoosh* of opening French doors onto a patio filled with golden light. The experience left me feeling conflicted. Although none of the places we saw inspired me, I felt a desire to please my partner and look at property with him. I didn't want that money to be sitting in the bank, either, but to work for us.

When I meditated on our situation and asked and listened for the lesson, I heard, "Wait until fall," a resonating thought that filled me with a warm, expansive feeling. By contrast, when I called to mind going ahead right then with a real estate deal, I felt a contraction, a lack of harmony with my inner Spirit.

As it turned out, in the fall we got a call about a condominium—a great deal because of a significant price reduction. Situated on a beautiful street in Boston's Back Bay, the condo was configured in such a way that we'd be able to divide it into two units, making it an excellent financial investment. A few unusual signs further indicated that waiting had been appropriate. The previous owner had left behind an astonishing number of little angel statues, as well as large paintings of angels; we also noticed several prints by the French artist Michel Delacroix hanging in the building's common space. We'd recently met Delacroix and really liked his work, and had, in fact, purchased a print.

The experience confirmed for me that when we're in attunement, life offers confirmation through feedback that a decision or action is, indeed, attuned. This doesn't mean that we're going to get all the information we need to make decisions right away. A while ago a guide told me, "When you're walking on the path of life and you see yourself coming to a fork in the road, that means you're going to need to make a decision, right or left." Often, the anticipation leading up to a decision can trigger anxiety, as people wonder, *Should I go right or left? What should I do?* My guide said, "The path on the way to the fork will give you more information—the information you will need to know what to do." Keep walking. . . .

CHAPTER TEN

Finding Wholeness

When you're having a hard time, go back to basics.

After my divorce, a good friend lived with us for a while. She loved my children, was fun to hang out with, and often provided me with intellectual stimulation. We supported each other in practical ways, too, exercising and meditating together every day and sharing in the preparation of quality meals. Her behavior was quite erratic, though, more than once calling to mind Longfellow's little girl with a little curl in the middle of her forehead: "When she was good / She was very good indeed / But when she was bad she was horrid." One moment she'd be singing and playing happily with my children, and the next she'd bolt out the front door in turmoil, upset by something she wasn't able to articulate.

When I projected my consciousness into her, and asked

and listened to gain insight into her fitful moods, I saw that she wasn't happy with how her life had unfolded, which caused her to feel bad about herself and reactive when things weren't going the way she wanted. I cared for her and enjoyed our friendship. At times, I felt desperate to help her. Finally, one afternoon, while sitting at my kitchen counter, I asked my guides to help me understand how feelings of inadequacy might be healed. The word I heard in response surprised me.

HUMILITY: AN UNEXPECTED ANTIDOTE

After that afternoon in my kitchen, I began to observe that many of my clients and students suffered from deep feelings of inadequacy. I asked my co-teaching guide why this affliction was so prevalent. He told me that the feeling of inadequacy is the number one "dis-ease" in cultures that emphasize competition over interconnection. Inadequacy, the feeling of being less than, he explained, is almost always an expression of a great desire to be accepted by and united with others. To genuinely fulfill this desire, my guide said, we need to get in touch with the spiritual principle of humility.

This instruction may sound counterintuitive at first. But early in my training, I'd been taught to meditate on words and concepts rather than to rely solely on dictionary definitions, as a way to gain experiential knowledge of their meaning and to develop an attuned use of language. So after listening to my guide's explanation, I meditated using the affirmation "I am filled with humility," repeating it a number of times. In the process, I discovered the experience of being one small, significant part of a whole, like a pebble on a beach or a leaf on a tree—a single drop in the vast sea of humanity. As I moved more deeply into that experience, I saw that each facet of the whole is as important as any other. In humility, there is no greater than or less than, no diminishment or self-effacement. There is simply an acknowledgment and appreciation of our particular role in the Oneness of all life, which precipitates profound feelings of self-acceptance, peace, and belonging.

I found applying this new understanding of humility to be simple yet extraordinarily effective. For years, I'd tried unsuccessfully to counteract my feelings of inadequacy by striving for excellence and recognition, but that tactic didn't provide me any emotional relief. When I was in school, for example, if I got a poor grade on a test I'd feel bad about myself and inferior to my fellow students. If I worked hard and achieved a good grade, I might feel better than others for a time, but even then my self-esteem was never stable. There was always the next test, the next grade, the next situation to worry about. My adult life was full of ups and downs, as well: financial tests, relationship issues, and the challenges and rewards of parenting.

But when I learned to focus inwardly on the spiritual principle of humility through repeating the phrase "I am filled with humility"—first in meditation and then more regularly throughout the day—I felt an increasing sense of peace, and a certainty that I was good enough regardless of circumstances. I no longer felt the need to prove myself in order to accept myself. I was still moved to grow and improve, but instead of being driven by fear, I was inspired to play my particular role to the best of my ability.

I realized, too, that in striving for excellence to antidote my feelings of inadequacy, I was following the precepts of modern Western culture. When we feel insecure, we're encouraged to work harder and either build ourselves up through "positive thinking" or allow ourselves to be built up by others—being told, in effect, "Hey, you're great!"

But if we don't genuinely feel good about ourselves, such efforts and encouragement usually don't penetrate. Most of us have probably experienced the ineffectiveness of this approach when dealing with friends, colleagues, or partners who feel inadequate. If we offer a compliment, they often can't take it in. If we're on the receiving end of the same sort of treatment, more often than not we experience, at best, only a fleeting boost in self-esteem. When inadequacy dominates our self-perception, what we actually need is to recognize that we are a "part of." The feeling of belonging, of being united with others, defuses insecurity by cutting through the sense of isolation that drives it.

There are a number of ways we can foster this recognition. For example, when my children were growing up, they often loved to hear stories about my own childhood mishaps and calamities. I've observed similar reactions among children of friends. Hearing such stories helps them see that they're not the only ones who do foolish things. It's a kind of humorous upside to the old adage "Misery loves company," a confirmation that we don't need to feel bad about ourselves, because we're not alone in our experience.

Sometimes taking active steps can help. Years ago, a client told me about her concerns for her adolescent daughter, who had very little self-confidence and consequently felt "emotionally shaky." Several months later, my client happily informed me that she'd begun to see a marked change in her daughter's attitude and behavior after the girl started volunteering at a soup kitchen. As she explained to her mother, her experience at the soup kitchen showed her quite vividly that she wasn't the only person who was struggling. It was clear to me that she had begun to internalize genuine humility. Feeling a common bond with others facing the challenges of the human condition, she gained a greater sense of inner tranquility and the confidence to seek a meaningful role in life.

CONNECTING WITH GREATNESS

Our culture's response to egotism is as misguided as our approach to inadequacy. When people feel and act as if they're better than others—belittling those around them, for instance, or persistently interrupting to assert their own views—we're encouraged to "bring them down a peg." According to my guides, however, people who strive for superiority are wrestling with a deep internal conflict. Disconnected at a conscious level from the genuine magnificence of their Spirit, they retain an unconscious remembrance of this innate grandeur. Longing to realize the potential they sense within, but confused by identifying only with what is commonly referred to as the ego—the limited, human aspect of their being—they believe they can feel powerful and significant only through dominating or outshining others.

This misconception, my guides explain, is the reason some people pursue recognition and achievement so aggressively. Their desire for prominence pushes them to excel, but success at the level of ego alone can never satisfy their deeper, subliminal yearning, and this frustration keeps driving them.

What they really need is to consciously connect with the greatness of their spiritual identity. If they access the pure source of their Spirit, the urge to feel superior dissolves, since the Spirit's magnificence eliminates the need to compare or compete. When people affirm the greatness of the self that lies within their Spirit and is united with all aspects of life, they affirm what is actually true rather than a distortion. From this state of connection, motivation changes from acquiring or increasing personal power to using strengths and abilities in ways that align with spiritual principles. Affirming and experiencing greatness because one is Spirit antidotes egotism.

For example, a while ago I had a conversation with the son of a client of mine. The young man, a teenager at the time, was extremely bright and consistently excelled in school. However, his mother was concerned that he was too ambitious and aloof, and, sensing an imbalance, she wondered if her son might benefit from some guidance. During our conversation, he mentioned that he often felt superior to his classmates and was driven to be the best in every class and in all his athletic activities. He believed this was the only way to achieve his potential, although he admitted that the emotional and psychological pressure caused him stress. His desire for what I would call "comparative greatness" meant that he didn't really want to be part of a group; he wanted to stand above and alone. Why, according to his way of thinking, would he *want* to be united with kids who weren't as capable as he was?

As I listened to him, it was clear that although he might suffer from the effects of isolation, he wasn't very likely to want or even be able to access humility. Instead, I acknowledged his talent and hardworking nature and emphasized, "From those who have been given much, much is expected." I suggested that he could direct his energy and drive toward becoming a positive and productive influence in our world and helpful to those who are less gifted and fortunate. My approach was twofold: first, to recall him to his genuine greatness, and then to emphasize the difference between compassionate, interconnected strength as opposed to competitive power. Our conversation evidently had some effect, because I later heard that he'd volunteered for a summer program devoted to building houses for disadvantaged people in a foreign country.

HUMILITY AND GREATNESS: TWO SIDES OF THE SAME COIN

When my guides asked me to teach a class on the relationship between humility and greatness, they told me that humility is like one side of a coin and greatness is the other. When these two principles are integrated, they explained, we experience a profound feeling of wholeness.

Greatness is a central aspect of our essence, the benevolent and loving power of the creator and essence of all life. When we get in touch with our fundamental greatness as Spirit, we access enormous potential. Think of a composer who receives music directly from a celestial source; a healer whose hands take away chronic pain; or our own ability to use remote viewing to gather knowledge. When we cultivate humility, experiencing ourselves as one small yet significant part of the whole of life, we accept our human limitations. Both our tremendous potential and our individual limitations are true at the same time, and when humility and greatness are balanced we dispel insecurity, isolation, and feelings of "less than" or "better than."

When we access our spiritual greatness we feel capable and influential—open to creative thinking and opportunities that benefit and strengthen everyone around us rather than using our strengths and abilities in ways that compete with, demean, or diminish others. When we connect with humility, we feel part of an interconnected whole that is always engaged in the process of learning and evolving, which is the antidote for inadequacy. In both situations, the attuned response is the opposite of what our culture has conditioned us to believe.

To demonstrate this point, in my class on humility and greatness I ask my students to reflect on a past experience when they felt inadequate. As they focus on that incident I tell them to repeat the affirmation "I am filled with humility" a number of times. Next, I ask them to observe how reviewing the incident while affirming the attitude of humility impacts the quality of the recollection. After that part of the exercise is complete, I ask them to recall the same memory, but this time using the affirmation "I am filled with greatness. I am one with all of life, the creator." Finally, I ask them to compare the two affirmation experiences.

As usual, I participate in the exercise along with my students. During one class, I focused on an incident that occurred when I was in fifth grade. I'd gone to a friend's house after school, and stood for a while with her and her older sister in their yard, looking at a pony in a corral. Turning to the older sister, I asked, "Do you ride the pony?" She replied,

"No." Then I said, for some unknown, stupid reason, "Are you chicken?" She simply said, "No, I'm too big." Boy, did I feel like a fool! Even though the event was years in the past, I still felt tense as I recalled it, but when I affirmed, "I am filled with humility," I relaxed and recognized that we are all foolish sometimes, which released the uncomfortable feeling of embarrassment.

When I recalled the scene once again, affirming, "I am filled with greatness," I discovered to my surprise that I didn't feel any sense of grandeur or expansiveness; in fact, I felt even more like a fool. The gap between the embarrassment and discomfort I'd experienced after my thoughtless remark and spiritual greatness was too wide to breach. The comparison between the two experiences confirmed for me that affirming humility really is the antidote to inadequacy, rather than affirming greatness.

After working with memories involving feelings of inadequacy, we turn our attention in class to occasions when we've felt superior. A man in one of my classes looked back to a period during the late 1990s, when he was convinced that anyone who didn't become wealthy during the dot-com bubble was stupid. Focusing on his feelings of egotistical arrogance, he went into meditation affirming, "I am filled with humility." In the discussion following this exercise, he told the class that reviewing his attitude from the perspective of humility had no effect whatsoever. However, he said, when he reexamined it while affirming his spiritual greatness, he found his arrogance transforming into a greater understanding that not everyone shared the same perceptions and abilities. He felt his whole demeanor soften, from a hard, judgmental stance to a kinder, more supportive disposition. Just as affirming my humility in my own experience of the exercise helped me get in touch with greatness, this man's experience of feeling his greatness helped him get in touch with humility—being a part of.

FINDING THE BALANCE

In meditating on the affirmation "I am filled with greatness," my experience and that of my students is one of vastness and benevolent power. It's often difficult initially for class participants to grasp that such strength and influence lie within them. Most have been conditioned to believe that they are "only human" and that the great universal force of creation is external—certainly not within them. Fully embracing the idea that each of us is one with the creator often requires intense or sustained meditation or some form of direct experience.

I know from my own experience, however, that with practice the effects of affirming greatness from a spiritual perspective can be swiftly and deeply felt. Years ago, for example, my companion and I were driving home from a vacation in Maine; I needed to use a bathroom and we decided to stop at a fast-food chain because of the company's reputation for having clean bathrooms. As I walked into the restaurant, I found myself slipping into a judgmental attitude toward the people eating there, thinking, "I would never eat that junk food." But because I'd recently taught a class on the relationship between humility and greatness, and because I do focus on self-observation—the "miniature me" over my shoulder—I quickly recognized the "better than" mind-set. I knew the antidote was to get in touch with my greatness, so I started concentrating on the affirmation "I am filled with greatness." After a few rounds of repetition my perception shifted. I no longer felt in any way superior; instead I felt connected to everyone and to the compassionate power of my Spirit, which roused in me a motivation to share knowledge about the importance of nutrition.

If I'd begun by affirming humility, I wouldn't have been able to arrive at that feeling of connection and compassion, because the gap between superiority and humility is too large to bridge. But once I felt the qualities of my Spirit, I was able to appreciate that I am human, too, learning just like everyone else. Once I applied the antidote of greatness, I could then access humility, attaining a balance that provided me with the feeling of wholeness.

Probably my most vivid and profound experience of the synthesis of humility and greatness occurred some forty years ago. I was driving home late at night when I noticed that my gas tank was low, so I pulled into a filling station. Just as I turned off the engine, I looked up and saw a clear and dramatic external vision. It was as if the roof of my Toyota station wagon had dissolved and in its place was an expansive sky with a classic image of an illumined, robed man with long, flowing white hair and a beard floating toward me, saying over and over again, "I am the universe." As he repeated this phrase, I became filled with its meaning and in that instant I, too, was the universe; I knew I was the creator of all life. At precisely the same moment, a man with greasy hands, dressed in stained coveralls, approached the car and asked me what I wanted. "Fill it up with regular," I told him.

These two experiences—so distinct yet so intimately

connected—occurred simultaneously. I was filled with the consciousness that I was the creator of all life. I knew that I had created the mountains and the seas—and the gas station attendant who was then filling up my tank with regular. I became acutely aware that the line between psychosis and enlightenment is very fine, but I knew I was on the right side of that line because I could count out my money and pay the attendant. I was able to hold both realities at the same time—to integrate and balance them—and drive away feeling I was definitely embodied as Ellen in a human form and at the same time I was one with all of life, the creator of the universe!

I believe many people experience being transported into a state of consciousness in which they experience being the creator, but in the process they lose contact with their human aspect. When this happens, they're often considered crazy or diagnosed as having suffered a psychotic break. What they're experiencing is actually something very true and real; unfortunately for them, the experience of being the creator, the all-powerful Oneness, hasn't been integrated with the recognition that they are simultaneously one small creation—a vulnerable, and very human, individual.

When we successfully integrate humility and greatness, we deepen both our understanding of our essence and potential as Spirit and our acceptance and acknowledgment of our individual experience of the human condition. Conscious awareness is the key to achieving this integration. When I'm teaching or lecturing, it's become automatic for me to consciously acknowledge that I am Spirit and human. And yet the freshness of experiencing myself as one small, significant person, like everyone in the audience, and at the same time connected to the Oneness, through which I'm able to access knowledge that goes beyond my individual human awareness, never fades.

INTEGRATING HUMILITY
AND GREATNESS IN DAILY LIFE

I sometimes think of the "application" of humility or greatness as a tennis game. Throughout the day, we move through a stream of interactions, relationships, and feelings. Each experience is a ball in our court. Do we need to respond with a backhand or a forehand? Do we respond with humility or with the greatness of Spirit? Which principle do we need to emphasize in order to achieve or maintain balance, clarity, and attunement?

Self-observation is key. Remembering the "miniature you" over your shoulder can help, and of course, examining situations through the third eye is vital. As you move through your day, take note of those moments when you feel less than or better than. If the "ball" of inadequacy is coming at you, hit it back while thinking, "I am filled with humility." If the ball of egotism heads into your court, hit it back while thinking, "I am filled with greatness." Once you feel the antidote correct your imbalance, you can affirm, "I am filled with humility and greatness," as a way to experience a deep sense of wholeness. As you train your mind, you'll gradually start to recall the experience without needing to consciously rely on affirmations. The balance between humility and greatness as well as the feeling of wholeness can become self-sustaining.

Unfortunately, our cultural conditioning, which emphasizes

lopsided attitudes, is quite pervasive, creating a challenging environment in which to develop a balanced approach to living. Through their wisdom and compassion, my guides have, over the years, offered a variety of skills and practices designed to help correct our attitudes and to antidote faulty conditioning. We've explored a number of these already, but I'd like to introduce here another set of tools that I've found extremely useful in restoring a sense of wholeness and balance in my life.

DISCIPLINE

At an early stage of my spiritual education my guides told me that if I didn't become more organized and attentive to practical details of daily life, they would stop working with me. In many ways they finished parenting me, a job that hadn't been completed by my biological parents, because my mother was ill and my father needed to work outside the home. My younger brother and I were seen as the "wild kids" in our neighborhood. The reputation was not entirely undeserved: We enjoyed a lot of creative freedom but lacked the kind of close supervision other parents gave their children. Compounding this situation was the fact that my father was a self-made man; born poor and disadvantaged, he achieved success through his own hard work and thought we should be able to figure things out for ourselves, as he had. Alas, I needed more guidance and support than I received.

I remember a guide scolding me one day, telling me to pick up after myself. He emphasized that establishing order in daily life is essential for maintaining peace of mind, supporting quality relationships, and fostering creative development. I was told to cultivate discipline in three areas—body, mind, and spirit—as well as to organize my home environment.

Establishing discipline on the level of my body involved paying attention to my diet, exercising daily, and getting enough rest, fresh air, and sunlight—attending to every aspect of my physical being. As I focused on this area, I became more acutely aware that genuine discipline required careful observance of many details. Paying attention to my diet, for example, meant being aware of the food's quality, its nutritional value, the setting in which I ate, and the times I chose to eat. Exercising daily required incorporating a variety of activities such as yoga, walking, and weight lifting, which enabled me to use and strengthen different parts of my body. Bringing discipline to my mind meant engaging in activities such as reading, writing, contemplating, and communicating, all of which contributed to keeping my mind agile and responsive in the same way that varying my physical activities helped maintain my body's flexibility, poise, and balance. The spiritual disciplines my guides encouraged me to follow included practicing meditation and third eye focus, cultivating positive attitudes, and asking and listening—again making sure to embrace variety.

Over time, as I integrated these three areas of discipline I began to feel less fragmented and more emotionally stable, prepared for whatever might come along. For example, instead of maintaining only a vague sense of my financial situation, which only made me worry about money, I focused on the details. I carefully examined my accounts to become clear about how much money was coming in and what all my expenses were. That precision provided the foundation I needed in order to avoid living beyond my means. On Sunday nights, I'd make a menu for the week, and on Monday morning I'd purchase only the items necessary for those meals, making sure I didn't exceed my budget. Creating this disciplined structure allowed me to get through a financially hard time without going into debt. In fact, one day a guide said to me, "When you're having a hard time, go back to basics." The basics, he explained, are the disciplines of the body, mind, and spirit, as well as the disciplines that bring order to daily living.

The particular way in which we incorporate discipline in different areas of life varies from person to person. For example, exercising in the morning and reading at night serves my schedule better than reading in the morning and exercising at night. Others may feel better served by a different approach, exercising at the end of a long day as a way to relieve tension, or reading inspirational material in the morning to set the tone for the day. In addition, many people find it easier to develop discipline in one area than in another. For some, physical discipline is more immediately rewarding than mental discipline. For others, reading, writing, and other kinds of mental discipline require less effort than setting aside time for meditation or other spiritual practices. It's unlikely that anyone will find cultivating discipline in all three areas equally manageable or equally challenging. No matter how your particular experience unfolds, the guiding principle according to my guides is the same: Don't avoid the areas in which your resolve is weak. Dive into them and they will become your greatest teachers.

This principle proved especially helpful to a former client who had gotten stuck in a situation I refer to as practicing "selective discipline." The structure she'd enjoyed during her school years had prepared her well for the mental disciplines of reading, writing, communication, and completing projects, and her positive early childhood memories of attending church services—supported by a strong spiritual orientation in many of her past lives—enabled her to easily immerse herself in spiritual practices. However, when it came to taking care of her body, she rebelled.

Her mother was a yoga teacher, a pioneer in promoting yoga philosophy and practices in the United States. Because of certain conflicts with her mother in this life and in past lives, she acted out by eating junk food, refusing to exercise, and gaining an unhealthy amount of weight. As we worked together to round out her approach to discipline, she was able to uncover several deeply buried emotional blocks, including feelings of not being accepted by her mother, as well as being unable to accept herself. Of course, these emotional issues could have surfaced by approaching them in a more direct manner. But the fact that they emerged indirectly—by her diving into her resistance to physical discipline—was significant, for she not only was able to discover a more balanced approach to discipline but also made progress in healing her relationship with her mother.

Some people resist discipline altogether, thinking of it as a kind of straitjacket. In fact, I've found—as many of my students and clients have, as well—that discipline actually provides a structure that allows us to be remarkably inventive. There are innumerable examples, such as mastering a new language before a trip abroad, taking a class in drawing or painting, or perhaps learning to play the piano or guitar. The order that discipline brings can also settle us and restore our sense of being centered. When we're out of balance and can't quite focus on what we should do, we can bring clarity into our life by directing our attention to completing some simple, mundane task. Do the laundry or wash your car. Take that long walk you may have been putting off because "there just isn't time." When I'm out of balance, my guides say, "Clean the house."

Of course, we all experience resistance to some disciplines at times. Let's say you decide you're going to exercise every morning. Then you wake up one morning and there's this resistance. "I'd rather go back to bed," you say. Or maybe you say, "Oh, I don't have to do it today." In my case, I find that if I put on my running shoes when I get up, I'm more likely to get out the door for my morning walk. When we repeat actions over and over again, they become habits, which are easier to sustain because they become part of our lifestyle. I'm also a big advocate of using props to help us move through our resistance to activities that reinforce our well-being—stylish exercise clothes, comfortable office furnishings, or candles for meditation and focus.

But even though we can minimize resistance, we need to remember that simply living on earth takes effort, an inescapable fact of the human condition. Walking requires effort. Eating requires effort. Even meditation requires effort. Cultivating discipline in the material world is a matter of consciously and consistently attending to what is needed in order to maintain physical existence and fulfill our spiritual purpose here.

However, sustaining the effort of living in the material world becomes drudgery if we don't enliven it with Spirit and its qualities.

SPONTANEITY

Embodied in the material realm, we're limited by physical laws and misconceptions of what is "humanly possible." In the spiritual realm, we experience the freedom of being un-limited: capable, for example, of traveling via thought alone. Spontaneity—the ability to pursue alternatives or act cre-atively within a structure, to follow impulses—brings us in touch with the unfettered liberty we enjoyed in the spiritual realm and long to regain. Perhaps you've noticed how children, newly returned to earth from the outer realms, are completely spontaneous and must be taught discipline to sustain a human life. Sadly, on our journey to adulthood, our innate sponta-neity often succumbs to the pressure to conform to cultural norms and social expectations.

This doesn't mean that our capacity to think and act cre-atively and independently can't be revived and nurtured when given the same attention as we devote to cultivating discipline. In fact, my guides emphasize that spontaneity is essential to fulfilling our purpose in incarnating on earth—which is to learn, to contribute, and to enjoy. Keeping the spark of spon-taneity burning stimulates our curiosity, our love of learning, and our willingness to be involved in the life around us. Spon-taneity rejuvenates us, too, providing the energy we need to sustain the effort of living in the material world without be-coming defeated or depleted.

The liberating, creative, and joyful feeling of spontaneity can be expressed in many ways. It's changing direction in midstream, being responsive to what's happening and open to unexpected feelings and changes. It's taking time away from completing a mile-long to-do list to connect with someone you meet unexpectedly on the street or in the grocery store. It's following the impulse to explore and learn something new even when doing so isn't part of your plan for the day, adding an enjoyable dash of variety to an already existing structure.

I remember reading an article not too long ago about a woman who, following the birth of her first child, had begun to feel isolated from her friends. She kept looking back at the simplicity and ease of just hanging out with them in high school and college, and all the fun they'd had together. Now that she was officially "a grown-up," whenever she and her friends were able to get together, it was usually for a formal dinner party—which took a lot of work and wasn't nearly as relaxing or enjoyable. One day, when her husband was out of town on a business trip, as an affirmation of spontaneity, she threw a bedsheet over her dining room table, called some friends, and invited them to come over that night for a potluck dinner. They had a fabulous time.

Too often, people think that enjoying a bit of spontaneous fun means laying out a lot of money. That's hardly necessary. When I was first married, in my early twenties, our finances were extremely tight. One evening my husband and I thought it would be fun to go to the movies, believing it was dollar night. When we arrived at the theater we discovered we were mistaken. So we decided to buy popcorn and sit on a bench, turning watching people into our movie experience.

BALANCING DISCIPLINE
AND SPONTANEITY

My guides say that cultivating both discipline and spontaneity is vital to experiencing enjoyment and stability in daily life. Discipline corresponds to having our feet on the ground, being firmly anchored, or grounded, in the particulars and necessities of living in the material realm. Spontaneity is the equivalent of the head-in-the-clouds experience of being connected to the expansive, spacious, and buoyant feeling we aim for when opening the crown chakra in meditation. Discipline involves taking responsibility, refraining from taking unnecessary risks, developing a routine, maintaining order, attending to details, and being consistent. Spontaneity includes expressing creativity, having fun, and being flexible, carefree, and open to the unexpected.

It's important to balance both qualities. Discipline without spontaneity is rigid, which leads to frustration, since life is filled with unexpected events, interruptions, and changes. Spontaneity without discipline is irresponsible and potentially dangerous. It can lead us to overextend financially or physically, or to take chances that may not be aligned with our own or others' best interests. When discipline and spontaneity are properly integrated, we form the synthesis of freedom and structure, destiny and choice, limited and unlimited, the human and the Spirit. We become steady and responsible, happy and invigorated, able to function harmoniously in groups and equally capable of standing alone.

The power of integrating discipline and spontaneity is perhaps most obvious in the arena of artistic expression.

Consider, for example, a dancer or a musician who is creatively gifted and expressive but lacks technique. After a while, such a performer can begin to wander off track, or fail to fulfill the promise of his or her artistic gift. Genuine artistry that keeps an audience engaged stems from integrating the structure of discipline with the creativity of spontaneity.

The same principle holds true in every aspect of life. Some time ago, I read about a cabdriver who decided if he were to be successful, he would need to make his job fun. To do this, he went about transforming his work situation. He bought a first-rate sound system and a wonderful collection of music; he also invested in a wide selection of magazines and books, which he read in order to encourage stimulating conversations with his fares. In other words, he used discipline to create a structure that offered him—and his passengers—a great deal of delight and spontaneity, because the situation was always rich and changing. He went so far as to print up business cards as people began to ask for him, and he became quite popular and successful. In short, through synthesizing discipline and spontaneity he transformed a job that could easily be considered drudgery into a joyful ride.

INTEGRATING DISCIPLINE AND SPONTANEITY IN DAILY LIFE

My guides emphasize that synthesizing discipline and spontaneity doesn't mean flip-flopping between one and the other—for example, working intensely for a year without a break and then taking a vacation. Instead, they advise learning to weave discipline and spontaneity together in day-to-day living. Some examples include exercising to music, cooking creatively, developing a schedule for a writing project that allows new ideas and creativity to flow, or inviting a friend to join you for a meditation session and discussing your experiences afterward. Life always contains a combination of fixed principles and varied expressions of those principles. When we synthesize discipline and spontaneity, we can learn to live in harmony with fixed spiritual principles while enjoying the endless variations of expressions.

Most people, my guides say, neglect this crucial area of personal development. They muddle through life in an ambiguous gray zone, enjoying neither the full freedom of spontaneity nor the strength and stability of discipline. Thoreau described such people in his classic book *Walden*: "The mass of men lead lives of quiet desperation. . . . A stereotyped but unconscious despair is concealed even under what are called the games and amusements of mankind. There is no play in them, for this comes after work. But it is a characteristic of wisdom not to do desperate things."

Some of my students worry that they may be slacking off when they feel too tired to exercise or too busy to meditate: Is this resistance, they wonder, or practicality? I encourage them to use the tools they've learned, such as asking and listening and viewing the situation through the third eye, to gain insight into their particular situation. Even taking the time to use these skills is an expression of spontaneity, a departure from the structured path for the day. It's also a wise approach to attunement in daily life.

There are times in my own life when, for some reason or another, I don't exercise in the morning as I'm accustomed to doing. Instead of dropping physical discipline altogether for that day, maybe I'll go for a walk in the afternoon, or put on some music and dance. Those are just a couple of examples of expressing spontaneity within the structure of discipline. Because physical, mental, and spiritual discipline can take many forms, spontaneity can be integrated with discipline in endless ways.

As with maintaining and integrating humility and greatness, self-observation can help you to strike the appropriate balance between discipline and spontaneity. Discipline sustains the human connection, the feeling of being "at home" in the body. Spontaneity brings a spiritual connection. If you feel dull, you need more spontaneity; if you feel unstable, you need more discipline. In many cases, meditating with the simple affirmation "I am filled with discipline, and I am filled with spontaneity" can help you become familiar with the feeling of the synthesis.

Discipline and spontaneity are powerful principles, so as you begin to work with them, a bit of caution is advisable. Over many years of working with students and clients, I've observed that some people fall back on discipline to avoid doing what they want to do but are afraid to try. I worked with a woman who was a frustrated artist. What she needed was to sit down and paint—to do the work she aspired to achieve. Instead, as she told me, "I do a lot of laundry." Some people who are disciplined clean their house a lot, but what they really feel they need to do is sit down at the piano or a writing desk, or maybe they meditate when they know they should be attending to their bodies.

In such instances, people let themselves be blocked by what I call "the inertia of fear." To work through this sort of block, it can be helpful to create a checklist—either mentally or written out—to determine whether you're being overly disciplined in one or more areas at the expense of the others. If the inertia of fear is causing you to neglect something you should be doing for yourself, dive into your resistance to gain insight and an attuned strategy for achieving balance and wholeness. As a guide once said to me, "Be as disciplined as you can be and as spontaneous as you can be."

CHAPTER ELEVEN

Attunement, Attunement, Attunement

Attunement is the only rule.

No matter how routine or predictable our lives may seem on the surface, no aspect of human experience is ever completely consistent or secure. As the nineteenth-century philosopher Thomas Carlyle wrote, "To-day is not yesterday: we ourselves change; how can our Works and Thoughts, if they are always to be the fittest, continue always the same?"

For many people, the evolutionary nature of life evokes fear, as well as the temptation to avoid facing or to repress the inevitable uncertainty of change. Attunement offers a positive and practical approach to working with the challenges we all must face, for in aligning our conscious mind with Spirit, we open ourselves to the full power and potential of the one and only unchangeable aspect of our nature. An attuned state of awareness affords us not only specific insights but also the flexibility to respond—in our thoughts, words, and actions—in the "fittest" or most appropriate way to the wide variety of situations we're likely to encounter. On a day-to-day basis, these may range from the personal and mundane, such as deciding what to have for dinner or handling financial or health concerns, to global problems of violence and climate change. Through practicing skills such as meditation, third eye focus, asking and listening, and cultivating positivity—and integrating these skills into daily life—we develop the expanded perception necessary to wisely navigate all aspects of our lives.

Attunement gives us the courage to move past avoidance and repression, and the clarity to see beneath turmoil and confusion precipitated by commonly held preconceptions. When we begin to disentangle ourselves from cultural norms and expectations—as well as from our own first-error fears and limitations—we become more adept at living consciously from the integrity of our Spirit, making choices that support our own and others' spiritual evolution. As my guides say, "Don't conform or rebel; rather, be the one who listens fully to Spirit."

Attunement is always situational. Once we step beyond rigid dichotomies of right or wrong and good or bad, we discover that there are no fixed rules or predetermined ways to respond to a particular event or set of circumstances. Sometimes strong action and outspokenness are required; at other times, a gentle, nurturing approach. Sometimes simply asking someone, "How may I help?" is the attuned choice. As a guide once said, "Be like nature: gentle like a zephyr, intense like a hurricane. Bend like a willow; stay steady like an oak."

Although spiritually attuned responses may vary, they always reflect a willingness to fulfill one's part and role in the larger orchestration of life, rather than an attempt to control and manipulate conditions to satisfy only personal, short-term desires. I've found in my own experience that following attunement allows situations to unfold in unique and surprising ways, encompassing interconnected intricacies that my analytical mind could never figure out on its own. Additionally, because a spiritually attuned route is frequently circuitous—filled with unexpected twists and turns as well as opportunities to meet the challenges linked to life lessons—I often find the ways in which circumstances develop more fascinating than a novel or a movie.

One striking example occurred a few years ago, when I needed to find an office space in Boston. During the years I lived in the country, I'd worked out of my home, a very convenient situation for a mother raising two children. My commute, a short walk across my mudroom to my work space, was fabulous. However, when I moved full-time into Boston in 2009 I needed to rent an office that was separate from our apartment. To meet the criteria I'd set, it had to be an aesthetically pleasing space within walking distance of my apartment, with steam heat and low overhead. As I scanned various listings, I noticed an ad for an office on Newbury Street, an elegant Back Bay thoroughfare and my number one choice. The real estate agent who showed me the space told me that the rent was two thousand dollars a month, an amount that far exceeded my budget. The figure I'd heard in meditation was two hundred; when I mentioned this number, the agent just laughed, saying, "You'll never find anything on Newbury Street for that price!" When I returned home and examined the experience through my third eye, it became clear that my next step was to wait. My guides often say, "All the data isn't in yet."

So I sublet a furnished office for two days a week in a beautiful building on Newbury Street, until more details revealed themselves. Not long afterward, I learned that an office was available, two floors down in the same building. Instead of going through a broker, I contacted the building owner, who showed me a large office with a small adjoining room that had its own separate entrance. Probably because the work space had been empty for more than a year, when I suggested that I'd be willing to rent the smaller room if a wall were installed to separate the two spaces, the owner readily agreed. She told me that every office in the building was rented by the square foot; after doing the math, I realized that my new rent would be two hundred a month. I had bookshelves built on either side of an impressive oak desk, brought in two wingback chairs, and decorated the walls with soothing prints. And of course my new office had steam heat!

STAYING CURRENT

When my guides first started teaching me about attunement, they directed me to review my experiences at the end of each day, neither repressing nor avoiding anything uncomfortable, as a way to refine my awareness. At the same time, I was instructed to make mental corrections when my thoughts, words, and actions were not appropriate for a given circumstance. Identifying these corrections, they explained, would help me learn to distinguish between attuned responses and those that were not in alignment with spiritual principles. The phrase they used to describe this nightly practice was "staying current." "Stay current with your communications," they advised, "with your decision making, and with the processing of emotional lessons."

After my children were asleep, I would sit in bed with my eyes closed and conduct my review, reflecting on both my inner and outer experiences from the perspective of my third eye. The process was surprisingly quick; I was able to scan the previous twelve hours or so, and watch while my imbalances leapt to the forefront of my mind for examination. When my thoughts, words, or behavior were reactive—a solar plexus response, either holding back or pushing for a result—I was guided to ask myself, "If I had been focused in the third eye in those circumstances, how would I have felt and behaved differently?" Then I envisioned the corrections.

For example, one night I reviewed a private session with a long-term client. I saw in my interaction with her that I'd felt impatient and attached to her getting herself together—developing more discipline and self-honesty and moving away from the pattern of blaming others for her issues. As I observed the way I'd counseled her, I noticed that my negative attitude manifested in my tone of voice, triggering in her feelings of shame and inadequacy. From my third eye perspective, I saw that while my insights were accurate and appropriate, my delivery was off. Had I maintained third eye focus more consistently during our session, I wouldn't have felt frustrated and attached to my client learning her lessons more quickly. Even in the review, this change in perspective opened my heart toward her; I imagined speaking more softly and kindly. I was also able to discern that I'd been physically tense, pushing rather than being aligned in my body. My correction involved both an attitude change and visualizing a physical adjustment. The next time we met, I put my observations into practice, and as a result our session was much more fruitful.

Sometimes, when attunement means to take a certain action or initiate a frank conversation, we may hesitate—perhaps out of concern over the other person's reaction. In such cases, my guides say, "You may need to wait for the right time to come around again." When an opportunity is missed, they advise, reexamine the situation through the third eye, and ask and listen to determine whether conditions are still appropriate. In other words, if we hold back from an attuned response, we shouldn't just make up for it by pushing ahead. Attunement is a moment-to-moment alignment. Just because we've received a clear insight into a situation doesn't mean it's still applicable once time passes.

Ultimately, staying current involves far more than ac-knowledging a mistake and hoping to do better next time. It's an integral part of the process of learning to master the dance of life. When we live in attunement, the experience is one of flow, moving with life as it unfolds, without pushing or holding back. This state is neither dependent on what other people do nor contingent on the state of the world. It's a practical and profound inner alignment with the spiritual Oneness.

CORRECTING IN THE MOMENT

I no longer practice the same detailed review every night, but that training helped me hone my self-observation skills. It also sensitized me, so that when my attitudes or behavior aren't attuned in a given moment, I'm more conscious of the discrepancy—usually in time to make a correction before I get too far out of balance. I have to smile sometimes when I recall an occasion, many years ago, when a guide said, "Once you live in the balance of your own being . . ." Before he even finished, my thoughts interrupted with a huge reaction: "That's never going to happen!" Now I do know what sustained emotional balance feels like, and I credit the nightly review process as the key to my learning.

In addition, that training taught me to ask frequently throughout the day, "Given what is, what am I to do?" Consistent inquiry is essential for sustaining attunement, particularly because seemingly unimportant choices or omissions can sometimes have serious unforeseeable consequences—a point vividly described in a poetic proverb that dates back to the fourteenth century:

> For the want of a nail the shoe was lost,
> For want of a shoe the horse was lost,
> For want of a horse the rider was lost,
> For want of a rider the message was lost,
> For want of a message the battle was lost,
> For want of a battle the kingdom was lost,
> And all for the want of a horseshoe nail.

I remembered this short poem recently, when I'd stayed on the phone too long. My companion was on a road trip across the country, and he called me early one Saturday morning as I was preparing to leave for class. It was nice to talk with him and he had interesting stories to tell, but I didn't leave myself enough time for my yoga routine, an important part of my morning—especially when I know I'm going to be sitting a good part of the day.

I could have said, very nicely, "I'll call you when I get home from class." Then I wouldn't have cut into the time I'd set aside for yoga, but because I held back from telling him I needed to go, when I got off the phone I started to feel tense and rushed to make up for lost time. Through self-observation, I recognized my imbalance and made a correction in the moment by deciding to perform the postures in my yoga series once instead of twice, as I normally do. This adjustment got me back into my flow and ready to teach my class.

In such situations, we might be tempted to think, "Well, that's a minor correction." But things have a way of snowballing when we don't apply even small adjustments. What happens in our day when we stay on the phone a little too long and our routine for the day is disturbed? We miss the flow in that moment, which can trigger unintended consequences down the line, leading to further complications.

In my case, it wasn't a big deal, but it's a good example of how staying current with moment-to-moment physical awareness can help us discern whether or not our choices are attuned. Take a moment to look back at an experience of being late for an appointment. Can you recall feeling as though your energy was ahead of your body as you rushed to get to the appointment? Or consider a classroom situation or a meeting at work when you wanted to speak up and express your thoughts but felt as though fear was holding you back. Both of these sensations—pushing or holding back—signal an imbalance. By contrast, feeling poised and centered in your body reflects an alignment, an attuned capacity to act or wait depending on what the situation calls for.

Staying current and making corrections can help us begin to discern patterns that keep us stuck in imbalance. A woman in one of my recent weekend classes shared that her husband—also one of my students—had suggested on the Friday night before class that they get up early Saturday morning and take their trash to the nearby dump before heading to the group. Explaining what had occurred, she told the class, "I said yes, but I kept thinking I had so much to do before we left for class. I knew that going to the dump would interfere with the priorities I'd already determined and would throw my balance out of whack. But I also knew we should get rid of the trash. When I got out of bed and started my day, and my husband said, 'I'll take care of the trash. You do what you need to do,' he seemed to know that going to the dump with him wasn't appropriate for me."

After a moment's reflection, she continued, "What he did put me back in the flow. He didn't let me make the mistake of pushing. It was such an amazing correction, because the rest of the morning unfolded easily and naturally. I accomplished what I had to do and we still got to class on time."

We decided to explore as a class what motivated her to say yes when the attuned response would have been no. As the discussion unfolded, it became clear that her impulse sprang from a deeply rooted misperception about personal responsibility: "If something has to be done, I should be the one to do it." Although she recognized that this view of her role in life was imbalanced and unsustainable, another question arose: How could such confusion come to rule her choices?

EMOTIONAL BAGGAGE

Emotions associated with long-forgotten experiences sustained in this life and previous incarnations can sometimes cause us to react to circumstances without knowing exactly why. However, as we become more proficient at staying current, we not only reduce the tendency to accumulate unresolved emotions but also begin to heal the confusion and fear lodged in our soul that have been carried over into this life. In the course of reviewing our thoughts, words, feelings, and actions through the third eye, we start to detect patterns: faulty attitudes and misperceptions whose origins we can begin to trace through asking and listening. As these become clear, we can apply appropriate antidotes. These may take the form of an attitude change, active steps that alter our behavior or situation, or a combination of both.

Sometimes we may be conscious of the origin of a particular fear or negative attitude but are still dealing with residual emotions. What do we do in such situations? My remarkably wise guides say, "Befriend the emotions and initiate a dialogue."

For example, many years ago, my dog, Mittens, got into a fight with a German shepherd. As I tried to separate them, the German shepherd bit my leg. It was a bad bite and for a couple of weeks I had trouble walking. For a long time afterward, whenever I was around a strange dog my leg would shake. I'd tell myself that the dog wasn't going to bite me, but my leg didn't seem to agree; the cells had their own consciousness and their own reaction to the memory. After asking and listening, I realized that reassurance was needed, so I began a dialogue with the fear in my leg. Every time I came in contact with a dog, I told my leg, "It's okay; I'll protect you. You can calm down." After a few weeks, the shaking stopped, and now my leg is no longer frightened of unfamiliar dogs.

Emotional baggage often accumulates around a first error. For example, I recently worked with a student whose first-error feeling of over-responsibility tends to snowball into a heavy burden of guilt. If she makes a commitment, she becomes distraught when circumstances change and fulfilling that commitment is no longer possible or appropriate. This sort of situation, I explained, usually requires a two-phase correction. The first phase, which might be called the "outer correction," involves calmly and clearly communicating that because circumstances have changed, it's no longer possible to fulfill a particular obligation. Of course, it's best to ask and listen before discussing the situation, in order to discern a wise way to frame the conversation.

The second phase is an "inner correction," which involves investigating the attitude that caused the problem in the first place. My student was holding on to a rigid definition of what it means to do the right thing, best summarized as "If I say I'm going to do something, then I *have* to do it, come hell or high water."

But as my guides say, "In life, spontaneity rules." Every moment is a creative unfolding, and we can't plan for every contingency. When doing the right thing is an attempt to override or control the spontaneous unpredictable aspect of life, we can become mentally and emotionally inflexible. It's physically impossible to please everyone, to always meet others' expectations, and to fulfill obligations when circumstances change. We have to adapt. Part of the transformation that occurs when we follow attunement is that we learn to change our language. Instead of saying to someone, "I promise I'll do it," we might say, "I'll take care of it." Then, if necessary, we can always go back to the person and say, "Well, I thought I could, but circumstances have changed. Something has come up that I need to attend to. How would you feel about taking care of this situation for me?"

The process of reviewing our experiences and learning to stay current teaches us that life really is a school and everyone and everything is part of our learning. As we make our own corrections, we discover that our relationship dynamics, our perceptions, and our choices evolve. At the same time, our curiosity is aroused as we wonder what's going to happen next.

BEFRIENDING ANXIETY

Recently, while in the waiting room of my dentist's office, I read a magazine article about a woman who depends on medication to alleviate her anxiety. I was particularly struck by her comment, "Everyone I know takes medication for anxiety." As I reflected on this remark, I thought about all the ads in magazines and on television that promote medication as a quick and easy fix for anxiety. When I returned home I asked in meditation for insight into why anxiety is so pervasive in modern culture.

A guide explained that anxiety is the turmoil brought on by fear. Its prevalence stems from a long-standing cultural emphasis on filtering experience though the solar plexus, which makes us susceptible to emotional volatility or becoming overwhelmed when circumstances fail to meet our needs, expectations, or desires. Instead of directly addressing the underlying fear and turmoil, however, many people choose avoidance and distraction as a superficial way of dealing with problems that appear to have no easy solution. Unfortunately, avoidance only compounds the situation, further embedding unresolved emotions and shaping our attitudes and behavior at an unconscious level. If a whole culture persists in avoidance, the problems don't magically go away. They multiply, creating an emotional environment in which the majority of people become reactive.

From my guides' perspective, anxiety serves a very useful function. It's a red flag, a signal that something is "off," and we need to pay attention because a change is needed. It may be a modification in attitude or behavior, a comprehensive change in the way we care for our body, or adjustments to any number of specific aspects of our life. Like a barometer, anxiety measures pressure and forecasts change. If we simply treat it with medication, we are, in effect, neutralizing its usefulness. The attuned approach—as with dealing with guilt, fear, and other emotional baggage—is to befriend anxiety, establish a dialogue with it, ask and listen. Allow it to become a teacher, pointing out what you're trying to avoid or the change you need to make in your life.

Since anxiety is often a highly charged emotion, the best way to approach this sort of dialogue is to begin by stilling your mind and opening up to your Spirit through meditation. Take a moment to focus on something that inspires you, that expands the crown chakra and prepares you for meditation. Once you feel the expansion at the top of your head, affirm, "I am

Spirit; I am infinite Spirit." Use the affirmation as much as you need it and let it go when you don't. If you're having trouble silencing brain chatter, you can mentally rock back and forth, repeating, "I am Spirit; I am infinite Spirit," and pausing, gradually lengthening the pauses between repetitions.

Once your mind is still, choose an issue that triggers your anxiety, project your consciousness into it, and begin a dialogue. There are any number of ways to initiate the conversation. You could, for example, simply say, "Anxiety, I'd like to befriend you and let you teach me." Or you might ask specific questions: "How do I resolve you?" "Do I need to change my attitude?" "Do I need to change my situation?" "Do I need to get help?" You might also ask, "What do you want to teach me?" "What actions should I take to mitigate you?" "Are you rooted in previous lives?"

Because anxiety can be quite dense and heavy, having this type of conversation helps to lighten it up and begins a process of releasing the blockage accumulated in the solar plexus. As the density begins to dissipate, we start to experience not only a sense of release and relief—particularly if we've been avoiding or repressing—but also a deeper awareness.

Through projecting into anxiety, we can receive insight into both its cause and the options available for healing and correction. According to my guides, it's important to feel the anxiety to learn from it and transform it. Sometimes this transformation can occur quickly—you've been working on it and working on it, and then it's just gone. Other times, it's more of a life lesson, and the answer you receive when you first begin the dialogue is only the next step in a larger process of learning.

For example, recently one of my students shared that she feels anxious almost all the time. "When I wake up in the morning, I'm shaking," she told the class. She went on to explain how she began using the tools she'd learned to examine and work with the feeling. "I went into the shaking, and what I got was that I'm afraid of being a person, of being in a body. When I asked what to do about it, the response I received was 'Realize that the anxiety makes you shrink, and embrace that you're human and shine. Love your life and embrace it.'"

As we discussed the answer she'd received, it became clear that the attitude change she was directed to apply wasn't a quick fix, because her anxiety was rooted in her first-error fear of not being safe in the physical world. Part of her lesson, therefore, was to focus on aspects of her life that were beautiful—to notice details and enjoy the gifts of her physical senses by studying the intricacy of a flower, for example, or listening to a piece of music. Weaving moments of simple pleasure into her life would trigger a sense of spiritual rejuvenation and help her remember that life on earth isn't just about struggle and strife but also about enjoyment.

Like any first-error fear, anxiety rooted in the fear of not being safe in the world takes time to heal. However, the attitude to correct and heal this particular fear is really quite simple: an acceptance of the fact that while our physical body is indeed vulnerable, our Spirit is eternally safe. Spending time in a group holding this perspective can help dissipate anxiety for a while, but sustaining the attitude needed to resolve anxiety based on first-error fears is often a lifelong practice.

Other forms of anxiety can be corrected—or at least diminished—by attention to detail. I've worked with people who feel anxious about their weight but avoid the scale and the day-to-day particulars of diet and exercise. When we allow ourselves to drift vaguely around the periphery of an issue, anxiety settles in or even intensifies. If, on the other hand, we rummage around, looking at the details, then we see "Ah, there's not really a problem" or "Oh, there *is* a problem and I need to attend to it."

RUSHING VERSUS RHYTHM

Many years ago, I was driving around the town near my home, feeling pressured to finish my errands before the stores closed. Suddenly, a guide came to me and said, "You have from now until eternity." As I absorbed the idea that I had enough time, I relaxed and moved into a feeling of flow. I discovered that rushing wasn't necessary to efficiently accomplish my tasks.

When I reviewed this experience with my guides, they explained that they make a distinction between rushing and rhythm. Rushing is an internal sense of pushing that causes stress and strain. Unfortunately, the tendency to rush is quite common in contemporary cultures, since so many demands are placed on our attention as we try to digest an overwhelming amount of information and multitask our way through a wide range of personal and professional needs and obligations. By contrast, rhythm emphasizes balance. We can move quickly or slowly in accomplishing a task, depending on what is called for, while simultaneously maintaining the feeling of equilibrium and flow.

Attunement can help us to refine our ability to discern whether it's appropriate to move through the day normally or approach a specific task in a leisurely manner or whether we need to pick up the pace. Using the third eye throughout the day to examine our physical sensations, thoughts, and feelings, and pausing to ask and listen, we can become more conscious of the feeling of flow, which confirms whether or not our actions and our attitudes are actually in harmony with our Spirit.

Of course, sometimes we need to step back and review certain experiences in order to discover why we are out of balance. For example, a student in a recent class described how, after waking up much earlier than usual, she started to read a book to pass the time before her first appointment of the day. Instead of stopping when the time came to prepare for the day, she kept reading a little more and a little more, until she knew she was running late. Even then, she lingered too long in the shower. By the time she finally left her house she was feeling cranky, and the internal imbalance extended throughout the day as she found herself unable to get back on schedule.

As we discussed her situation, I suggested that being late in and of itself isn't a measure of imbalance. Deviating from a schedule may be an attuned choice, for any number of reasons. Perhaps the people we've arranged to meet or speak with may be experiencing their own conflicts or delays, or by moving slowly we miss a traffic jam. As my guides explain, in order to make an accurate assessment, we need to look at the quality of our inner experience. Digging a little deeper, I asked, "When you kept reading the book, did you feel as though you were aligned, holding back, or pushing?"

She considered a moment before replying, "I started to feel pressure because I was sitting too long reading. But I just wanted a little bit more, because I was reading purely for pleasure." Reflecting further, she added, "I think that impulse to keep going is something that carried over from childhood, just sitting there reading a book until it's done. It's a habit."

This was an important discovery for her, as it has been for many of my students and clients, for habits often pose significant obstacles to attunement. When we're used to doing something in a particular way, that pattern—and the underlying attachment that holds it in place—can cloud our judgment and obscure our sensitivity to the demands of a particular situation. Reading a book until it's done may be a fine way to pass the morning on a beach during a summer vacation, but it's most likely not appropriate when you need to get to work on time, meet a client, or even join a friend for breakfast.

LOVE AND LOVING

My guides define *love* as the force that flows out of the spiritual essence. It is warm and unifying and makes us feel glad to be alive. They describe *loving*, the process of expressing this force, as acting in harmony with Spirit and its nature. In other words, genuine loving and attunement are really the same.

Our eagerness to give and receive love is as potent a force as our longing to understand ourselves. Our music, art, literature, and films all express this yearning. Yet despite the depth of this longing, even people who are purely motivated must work through fears, hurts, and misconceptions to achieve and sustain this sublime feeling. In order to fully and genuinely experience love, we need courage, clarity, and determination, for in our culture, ideas and attitudes about love and loving are confused and uncertain.

Part of the difficulty stems from cultural conditioning and expectations about relationships. Consider the misconception, which has been making the rounds for a while, that we need to love ourselves before we can love others. My work with students and clients has shown me this is simply not true. I've encountered a number of people who find it easier to love others than to love themselves. Ultimately, it doesn't matter whether our love is initially directed toward ourselves or others. Through loving another, we can generate self-love; through loving ourselves, we can develop love for others.

Another common fallacy is expressed in the complaint "If you really loved me, you'd do what I want." What people *want*, however, isn't always what they *need* in order to evolve. Unless we're vigilant in accessing clarity and confidence of Spirit through staying current and making corrections in our attitudes and behavior, we can easily give in to the belief that loving means giving people what they want, when in fact the lessons they need to learn may require something quite different.

Confusion around love and loving also comes from fear, which is built into relationships based on what I call the "barter system": "You meet my needs, and I'll meet yours." When we look deeply at this kind of arrangement, we can see that the partners in such a relationship are striking a deal rooted in avoidance and repression: "You keep me from getting too caught up in my fears, and I'll keep you from getting too caught up in yours." Such a relationship obviously isn't focused on mutual growth and learning.

Another fear-tinged scenario involves a person who says,

"Because I love you, I want to do this for you." For example, a friend of mine always wanted to give me presents. Her persistent generosity may have been partly inspired by love, but her primary motivation was a fear of being rejected or not included in my life.

I once asked a guide why so many people harbor the fear of not being loved, even though on a spiritual level everyone is loved. He explained that in the human condition, it's easy to succumb to the illusion of being a wholly separate individual, completely disconnected from others and from our fundamental spiritual identity. Although love is always present and active as a spiritual principle, it cannot be fully experienced or expressed until we recognize the Spirit within or the interconnected Oneness. In everyday practice, this means that when we commit ourselves to attunement in our relationships, "What is the loving thing to do?" and "What is the attuned choice?" are essentially the same question. Consequently, the answer we receive should be the same. When we are loving toward another person, we support that person's growth as well as our own.

In my classes, I ask students to use meditation and third eye focus to look at a past or present relationship and, through asking and listening, discern the loving choice in a particular situation. This exercise often demonstrates quite clearly how conditioned thinking about love and loving short-circuits the ability to determine a genuinely loving response. Conditioned thinking yields a patterned response, whereas an attuned insight fits the situation in all its specificity.

For example, a young man chose to examine the way he dealt with his wife's anger, which erupted recently when he brought up his concerns about her credit card use. At the time, he responded as he normally did, trying to soothe and placate her, a tactic he'd learned from watching his parents argue. Afterward, when he analyzed his response intellectually, he decided that a more appropriately loving response would be "to just sort of let the anger in and through, and not really respond at all." But after looking at the situation through his third eye and then asking and listening, he discovered that this approach—based on the idea that the loving choice means avoiding conflict—was just another form of the same conditioning. Ultimately, he realized that while he needn't take his wife's anger personally, neither should he allow her antagonism to prevent him from expressing his own perspective: that credit card debt was not a good idea, and that many of her purchases were not wise choices. He also saw that he could use his third eye wisdom to help him choose an appropriate time to initiate a candid conversation about their different approaches to money management.

As my students learn to identify the loving response in the different circumstances they explore in class, many begin to worry that they will not have the presence of mind or the time in everyday life to attune. Some of them express concern that they're liable to be too caught up in their own emotional reactions. One woman described such a situation in the story she told about a recent argument with her husband.

"He just got furious with me," she explained. "And I immediately got furious back at him for getting mad at me. I walked out of the room, and it caused an enormous fight, far beyond the issue that triggered it. I see now, after looking at the situation in class, that the loving response for me at that moment would have been to just stop when he got so mad at me and ask, 'What is going on with you?' That's what his Spirit was asking for, and that would have gotten to the heart of the issue. But it was hard for me to do it, because I was very wrapped up in my emotions about whatever it was. Attuning was the last thing in my mind."

Often, when trying to attune in the moment, we need not only to ask and listen, but to pause *before* asking and listening. Taking the time to pause gives us a chance to focus and move away from the impulse to react from preconceived ideas and images. For instance, a number of years ago I received a phone call from a friend who was struggling with her health. As I listened to her, I offered a suggestion that I thought might be helpful, but when I hung up, I decided to look more deeply into her situation. I stopped what I was doing and paused, which took very little time. My deeper insight was quite different from my immediate response: I saw that the loving choice was to invite my friend to our house for a few days in order to provide a healing space and some emotional comfort. When I called her back and extended the invitation, she felt relieved and replied that she'd hoped to spend some time with me at my peaceful home in the country.

INTERNAL AND EXTERNAL OUTCOMES

My guides have cautioned against judging the accuracy of an attuned response by feedback or immediate external outcomes. This point was driven home for me when, the day after I'd given a public lecture, I received a phone call from a woman who could scarcely contain her enthusiasm, going on and on about how my talk had helped her and what an inspiration I was. I thanked her and hung up the phone. A few minutes later, my phone rang again. This time it was a man who had attended the very same lecture. He was clearly upset, criticizing me for being irresponsible and declaring that I should never have publicly presented ideas that were harmful to people's psyches. I thanked him for his feedback and hung up the phone.

Almost immediately afterward, one of my guides said, "Do you see how you should never judge the value of your work by the feedback you receive? Someone may compliment you and be confused or insult you and be confused. Be the one who listens fully to Spirit."

This is an important point. In some cases, others may disapprove of our attuned choice. In other situations, if we don't see an immediate result, we might end up second-guessing ourselves, believing the attuned choice was wrong. If we withhold judgment and let time pass, we may discover that our attunement was exactly right. There have been times, for instance, when a client didn't respond well to our work together, or resisted what I had to say, but then years later I'd receive a thank-you note expressing deep, heartfelt appreciation.

Judging an attuned or loving response by the immediate outcome often indicates an unexamined desire to avoid conflict and achieve a short-term harmonious result. From this standpoint, if our choices initially lead to disagreement or tension, we may lose confidence in the attunement and focus instead on the behavioral outcome. This could happen, for example, when disciplining a child through establishing clear and appropriate limits about what is and is not acceptable.

Setting restrictions, although loving, may result in the child becoming angry, uncooperative, or disruptive in any number of ways. In the face of this conflict and disharmony, it may be difficult to stand firm. Yet establishing limits is a loving choice even if positive outcomes don't show themselves for a while and the immediate consequences appear negative. My guides say, "We are not interested in the short-term result, but rather the long-term result."

Choosing attunement—choosing to live more consciously with a more expanded perception—doesn't always transform the external circumstances of our lives. However, as we align our thoughts, feelings, and behavior with spiritual principles, we'll definitely begin to experience a deeper sense of inner balance, peace, and harmony. Sometimes it takes courage to live what we learn through attunement. We can't always predict whether our attuned response is going to be what we consciously desire or wish for. But as our awareness becomes more fully aligned with Spirit, our conscious intentions and the answers we receive through attunement become synonymous.

CHAPTER TWELVE

Perfection

Ignorance is in perfection also.

The nomadic artisans of the Middle East often deliberately wove a slight inconsistency into the richly patterned carpets they created. The Arabic word for such imperfections is *abrash*, which may have originated from a Persian term meaning "mottled" or "blemish." Sometimes referred to as a "Persian flaw," this irregularity in the color or the weave of a carpet is meant to acknowledge that only Allah is perfect, while human beings are prone to error.

I often use the example of the Persian flaw to illustrate a distinction my guides make between *perfect* and *perfection*. They describe Spirit, the essence of our nature, as *perfect*: complete, ideal, and flawless. *Perfection* is a process, an ordered, interconnected evolution toward actualizing Spirit's nature in both the etheric and physical form. Whether we're conscious of it or not, we are all involved in this journey. Sometimes our experiences along the way are painful; sometimes they're pleasurable. But as my mother articulated many years ago, "There are always reasons."

In deep meditation, from a place of no thinking, I've been able to feel the orchestration that my guides refer to as "perfection." I confess that when I return to a post-meditative state, it's hard to wrap my mind around the profound and intricately detailed order of Spirit's expression. Trying to intellectually grasp the immense scope of the evolutionary unfolding of perfection is like trying to fully and simultaneously understand every microcosmic and macrocosmic aspect of the universe—a feat well beyond analytical comprehension. Yet, in deep meditation, once we glimpse, even briefly, the perpetual movement of perfection, and its significance in our personal lives, we do see that no experience is irrelevant and no individual is excluded.

A RADICAL CHANGE

In my class series, I teach a lesson on the relationship between perfect and perfection. I begin by inviting my students to discover for themselves the difference between the words *perfect* and *perfection*. I ask them first to meditate using the affirmation "I am perfect," and then to meditate on the affirmation "I am filled with perfection." I ask them not to think about or analyze either concept, but instead to experience and observe the impact of each affirmation.

Many of them discover that affirming, "I am perfect,"

produces a sense of being fixed or locked in place. Some of them find it hard to even breathe. Without exception, they describe the experience of *perfect* as an end of movement and growth, an arrival rather than a journey. No change or improvement is necessary or possible.

From an ordinary perspective, the futility of striving to be perfect isn't hard to see. No matter how hard we try, we can never fully achieve a condition in which we're finished or complete. On a cellular level alone, change is inevitable. Relationships, work, even simple activities such as walking from room to room or eating meals—all require some degree of adaptation and movement. Being perfect is simply not possible within the context of the human condition.

By contrast, affirming, "I am in perfection," evokes in my students the sensation of being immersed in a progression of change and creative development. They experience a clear and dynamic sense of alignment with a cosmic force—very much like the power that propels rivers, streams, and tributaries to the sea. Being *in perfection*, they discover, allows them to begin to let go of conditioned habits of manipulating situations to achieve personal goals. Instead, they activate a motivation to consciously participate in this evolutionary flow of life.

As they shift their attention from trying to be perfect to an awareness of being in perfection, radical changes occur in the way they experience and perceive life. Attempting at a human level to be perfect in any aspect of life, they find, is stressful, since it's aiming for a goal that can never be reached. It also pushes them toward becoming self-centered, creating emotional disconnection and isolation. When they shift their awareness to being in perfection, physical and emotional stress diminishes, and they open to an acceptance and appreciation that the whole of life is supporting a process of learning and development in which everyone is involved.

THE WEB OF EVOLUTION

You can begin to experience such an awareness yourself in meditation and through a simple asking and listening exercise I offer to my students.

Still your mind in meditation, and then examine a recent event or situation. Recall the details, including physical sensations, thoughts, and any emotions you felt. Next, take a moment to still your mind once more and then ask, "What is the perfection of this situation?" The response you receive may surprise you.

In one of my classes, for example, a woman in her late fifties chose to examine an upsetting conversation with her sister, who had recently visited from another city. During the conversation, her sister pointed out that my student was too old to purse a PhD and insisted that she was wasting her time working toward an advanced degree that wouldn't lead to career opportunities or financial improvement.

Her sister's assessment initially felt devastating to my student. But when she reexamined the conversation from the perspective of perfection, she was able to see the love and concern behind her sister's seemingly harsh advice.

"I could feel it was no longer a win-lose situation," she told the class, "but rather a learning for me to hold on to my identity and clarity—even when my decision wasn't supported—as well as a chance to learn that we could stay close even if we didn't agree.

"Even more remarkably, when I looked at the situation from the perspective of perfection, I could see my sister's learning as well as my own. She had always seen herself as the 'smart one.' She'd received a PhD at a young age, and became a professor and an expert in her field. In my meditation, I became aware that my sister was projecting her situation onto me. With my ability to hold my own sense of identity, I was giving her an opportunity to see me and my situation, rather than generalize."

As it turned out, my client did earn her PhD and was hired as an adjunct faculty member at a local university. Not only did she realize her aspiration for wider career opportunities, but the combination of the pension she received from her previous job and her salary from her new position brought her financial stability as well.

But her story illustrates an even more important principle. Courageously accepting an attuned choice often creates a ripple effect that positively impacts the lives of other people, even those we may not ever know. My student's niece—her sister's daughter—had dropped out of college years earlier. But in her forties, partly inspired by her aunt, she went back to school and pursued an advanced degree. She became a teacher, and in the course of her work she touched the lives of many students— who, in turn, touched the lives of many others.

As my guides explain, perfection is a web. Our individual spiritual development ultimately contributes to the evolution of all humanity. When we ask, "What is my lesson?" we're focused on our individual learning as it relates to a particular situation. When we ask, "What is the perfection of this situation?" we're consciously choosing to expand our perception to include the far-reaching ramifications of our own learning and the growth and development of others.

When we look at experiences from the perspective of perfection, we begin to see this ripple effect—this flow of change and growth—across all lessons and circumstances. We are always, so to speak, in the hand of the compassionate force of Oneness moving us closer and closer to spiritual actualization.

From the interconnected perspective, we begin to develop a deeper and more vibrant attitude of curiosity. When an event happens—an interaction, a meeting, an experience—instead of judging it as good or bad, right or wrong, we begin to ask, "What does this lead to? What does this trigger? What does this cause me to initiate? What is its purpose, personally and collectively?" When we start to look at life this way, it becomes an adventure, rich with creativity and involvement.

For example, when my daughter was in fifth grade, the principal of her school called me into her office for a meeting. Essentially, she apologized for failing my dyslexic daughter, who at that stage of her education could hardly read. Although she'd been tutored for years and had memorized many rules, she was unable to apply them. The situation, already troubling, was aggravated by the fact that her classmates bullied her and called her stupid.

After years of fruitlessly seeking a solution, I received a phone call one afternoon from a woman named Elizabeth, who had recently moved to our area. "I've heard you're looking for help with your dyslexic daughter," she said. "I think I can help." She explained that she used to run a school in the Boston area for children with learning disabilities, so I invited her over for tea to discuss the specific assistance she could offer my daughter.

When she arrived, Elizabeth told me that she'd been trained in an approach known as the Tomatis Method. Alfred Tomatis was a French ear, nose, and throat doctor who found evidence that a number of learning difficulties, including dyslexia, resulted from impairments in the function of the middle ear that prevented listeners from hearing certain sound frequencies. He created a device called the Electronic Ear, which tones the muscles of the middle ear in order to sensitize the listener to missing frequencies.

Elizabeth explained that her discovery of the effectiveness of the Tomatis Method, and her decision to train in it, transformed her career. She abandoned the other approaches she'd studied to help children with learning difficulties in favor of the Tomatis Method. I thanked her for coming to speak with me, and after she left, I went straight into meditation. It didn't take long for me to hear one of my guides say, "This is what you have been waiting for."

I remortgaged my house and hired Elizabeth to homeschool my daughter for an entire year. I confess I was more than a little awed by the interconnected perfection of events. More than a decade earlier, I had been one of a small group of people who spearheaded a class action suit to legalize homeschooling in Massachusetts. Had we not followed the attuned decision to pursue legal action, my daughter might not have been able to benefit from homeschooling.

The Tomatis Method did prove to be the solution we'd sought. After one year of working with Elizabeth, my daughter advanced from hardly being able to read to reading at a seventh-grade level. Once her middle ear had been successfully trained, her natural intelligence caused her to soak up knowledge like a sponge. However, even though she'd made tremendous progress, it was clear that she would best be served by attending a middle school with small classes and a lot of support rather than an overcrowded public junior high school.

At this point, the ripple effect of the perfection of following an attuned decision became even more apparent. Because private school was expensive, I needed to expand my private counseling practice and my teaching options in order to earn enough to pay for my daughter's tuition. This required a significant emotional adjustment on my part, because I had to step outside the familiar comfort of working in an isolated, rural environment and seek out a larger number of clients and students. Despite my initial timidity, I began to work with a broader range of people, which ultimately served my growth as a teacher and a student.

But even as I dealt with the financial challenge and the prospect of overcoming my personal vulnerability, I had to reckon with another issue. Although there are many private schools in the valley where we lived, very few of them were middle schools. As I researched and spoke with headmasters, it became clear that only one school would embrace a dyslexic girl with my daughter's history—and only if she could pass the entrance exam.

Before my daughter was even scheduled to sit for the exam, we had to fill out an application, which included a writing sample. The sample she submitted was a story she'd dictated to a family friend earlier that year, describing a past-life experience as a black slave girl. The headmaster of the middle school she applied to was a gentleman who'd been born and raised in Zimbabwe. When we spoke to him a few weeks later, he told us that when he read my daughter's story he cried. He was so moved that a twelve-year-old white girl could emotionally understand the plight of a black slave that he admitted her without requiring her to take the entrance exam. During her time at the school, he took my daughter under his wing, frequently encouraging her by telling her that she was brilliant. As I reviewed the entire progression of events in meditation, it was clear to me that my daughter's journey offered a remarkable demonstration of my guides' description of perfection. While she certainly moved closer to actualizing the intelligence inherent in her spiritual nature, her evolution affected the lives of so many others—including her tutor, the headmaster of her school, me, and the clients and students I reached as I stepped beyond my own limitations.

EVEN IGNORANCE IS IN PERFECTION

Perfection doesn't always unfold in an obvious, orderly progression. In most cases, it takes a circuitous route, because it takes time to assimilate the lessons we need to learn. As my guides say, "It takes time for all the dominos to get lined up."

When we approach our experience from the perspective of perfection, we begin to see that everything that occurs—however painful, puzzling, or bleak—contains a hidden benefit, a useful meaning. This principle was summarized eloquently in Archbishop Desmond Tutu's observation about Nelson Mandela when the South African leader was released after twenty-seven years in prison. "Prison made the man," he remarked. "A fairly robust and aggressive young militant became a generous, understanding person."

My guides say that even ignorance is in perfection, because the choices we make without due consideration of the consequences set in motion a snowball effect of events that sooner or later lead to deeper understanding. For example, one of my students recently described a situation in which she'd been living with her sister in Vermont, when out of the blue her sister decided to sell her house and move out west to be closer to her children. Shocked by this abrupt turn of events, my student found, without much investigation, an apartment that seemed perfect. Not long after she'd moved in, her landlord called to inform her that he'd inadvertently placed her in the wrong apartment, which, as it turned out, was illegal, so she'd have to leave. The very next day, her employer, for whom she'd worked for six years, abruptly quit the company. All at once she found herself in an extremely unsettled situation: jobless, homeless, and bereft of any ties to her new community.

But instead of giving in to panic or blaming herself for making a hasty decision without fully examining the consequences, she decided to meditate on the perfection of her situation. As she looked at the way circumstances had unfolded, she saw an opportunity to move to New York to live near her children. The decision felt completely attuned. Within days, she found a place to live that felt peaceful and safe. She developed friendships with people in her new neighborhood and found some new clients who have helped her expand her career opportunities.

"The whole experience," she told the class, "has been tiring, but rich. I was able to remain strong and focused throughout, and now I feel happy with the turn of events."

Recognizing and accepting the perfection of ignorance helps us to cultivate trust in the larger orchestration of life. We're never lost, even if we feel like we are. There are always reasons why situations unfold as they do. When we ask, "What is the perfection of this situation?" we discover that even the choices we make out of ignorance actually move us closer to the actualization of our own spiritual nature and the spiritual evolution of others.

THE PERFECTION OF ADVERSITY

Even circumstances that appear challenging or adverse are in perfection. I was recently reminded of this when I watched Ken Burns's documentary *The Roosevelts: An Intimate History*, which chronicled the lives of three members of one of the most prominent political families in American history.

I was particularly struck by the contrast between the footage of Franklin Roosevelt before and after he contracted polio. It appeared to me that the extreme physical and emotional struggles he endured prepared him for the challenge of leading the United States through a worldwide economic depression and a consuming world war. The strength of character he developed in handling his personal adversity helped him sustain and communicate the optimism needed to support the American people during a period of great hardship.

After I watched the series, I asked my guides for their

perspective. They explained that Franklin Roosevelt was not perfect, but his experience exemplified the broad scope of perfection, for the challenges he endured as an individual rippled outward in ways that influenced the attitudes and actions of an entire nation, and extended in many ways around the globe. His empathy, which evolved through his intimate experience of suffering, may best be summed up in a remark he made during his second inaugural address: "The test of our progress is not whether we add more to the abundance of those who have much; it is whether we provide enough for those who have too little."

Yet, despite the efforts of people like Franklin Roosevelt, who have dedicated themselves to serving others, our world still seems to be headed toward greater suffering and chaos. And, like many people, I often find myself searching for a deeper understanding.

THE PERFECTION OF
GLOBAL TURMOIL

Is pollution in perfection? Is homelessness, or the cruelty and chaos of war? If every situation is in perfection then the answer to these and similar questions must be yes. But if everything is in perfection, why should we concern ourselves with the problems of the world? Why worry about pollution or global warming? Why recycle or drive a fuel-efficient car? Why concern ourselves with the accumulation of toxic waste on land or in the oceans, lakes, and rivers of the world?

My guides have helped me understand the perfection of

social and global problems by comparing them to physical illness. If our body is diseased, the perfection of that situation often points to lessons to be learned, or perhaps a balancing of the consequences of past-life attitudes and behaviors. For example, my mother's physical suffering helped her learn compassion. But her learning also triggered my own learning, as well as my father's and my brothers'. Similarly, social and global problems may be understood in broad terms as expressions of cultural "disease," which, seen in the context of perfection, offers opportunities for growth, learning, and balance on a societal scale.

The escalation of violence, the growing indifference toward those in need, and the blatant disregard for the welfare of the planet are all symptomatic of a collective disconnection from our spiritual nature. The extreme situations we face today are warning signs. If we heed them, they can motivate us to examine more deeply who we are and why we've incarnated on earth at this time. Unfortunately, it does seem that the challenges we face on a global scale—the devastating effects of climate change, the horrors of sectarian warfare, the mass murder of schoolchildren and other innocents—have to rise to a critical level before we finally begin to pay attention. Like cigarette smokers who quit only after they've been diagnosed with lung cancer, most of us are moved to action only when the conditions of our world beg for change.

We can see in our own lives and in the events unfolding around the world the ramifications of continuing to avoid, repress, or allow ourselves to become overwhelmed by negativity. If we don't learn from one calamity, then another occurs. And if we don't learn from that, another catastrophe follows. The "disease" progresses until we finally make a conscious choice to learn to actualize our spiritual nature.

This progression, from suffering to acceptance to actualization, is perfection at work on a grand scale, an interconnected process of evolution from which no one is exempt. More than forty years ago, my guides told me that our world situation would worsen—the inevitable result, they explained, of the destructive attitudes and actions arising from first-error misconceptions. Ultimately, though, our individual Spirit, supported by the positive forces in the spiritual realms that hover around us, and the infinitely wise and loving Spirit that infuses all creation will awaken us to a remembrance of our true nature—whether we consciously embark on the road toward manifesting spiritual principles here on earth or after we return to the spiritual realm.

THE INFINITE VIEW

I once asked a guide if the lessons we learn through embracing perfection will eventually lead us to return to Oneness and eliminate all individuality, restoring us to a condition that existed before the Big Bang. He advised me not to worry about possibilities that may unfold in the distant future. Instead, he suggested that I focus my efforts on actualizing my spiritual nature with consistency.

"There is a plan on earth," he explained. "All people are part of this. You can choose to flow with this expectation or not. If you choose not to, there is no loss, for there is always the opportunity to learn and deepen and grow. No matter what you choose, you cannot step out of the perfection of the flow of the Spirit, for it is everywhere. It is by the conscious choosing of flowing with it that you step into the certainty of your own identity and the vibrational flow of life. This step ceases the struggle and brings about the surrender to the spiritual forces that are the essence of life itself.

"The difficulty," he continued, "comes in the integration of spiritual concepts with the human expression. For it frequently appears that there are many contradictions in human experience—good and bad, joy and sorrow, struggle and ease. As you enter into the spiritual Oneness, these dichotomies cease. You learn that Oneness is still the rule. For it is in the attunement to the Oneness that the understanding of the manifestation of this perfection in form is realized."

I recalled this remarkable teaching while sitting in a restaurant waiting for a friend to join me for lunch. As I gazed out the window I noticed two disheveled, unhappy-looking people sitting on a bench across the street. I remember thinking, "How are these people going to find a way to actualize their spiritual nature? I'm working so diligently and consciously at this process. Even with all the advantages I have, it's not easy for me—and these two seem to be much more challenged."

Suddenly, a vision appeared in the sky of angelic beings with golden horns, heralding all humanity upward into light. The scene reminded me of certain medieval paintings I'd seen in museums, depicting masses of people entwined in a spiral of interconnection. As each person moved into the light, everyone else was drawn up, for they were all intertwined. No one could be excluded because no one was separate or isolated.

I realized in that moment that when any one person

actualizes his or her Spirit's nature, the effects ripple out across all humanity. Every attuned choice we make contributes to the larger orchestration of spiritual evolution.

As the vision faded, I heard a guide say, "When living in attunement, your personal spiritual attainment is simultaneously your service. Do not serve the individual. Do not serve yourself. Rather, serve the Oneness of which you are a part."

ACKNOWLEDGMENTS

First, I would like to extend a heartfelt thanks to my many students and clients who throughout the years have provided me with the laboratory to test and demonstrate the teachings of my guides.

Second, I want to acknowledge that without the sensitivity and writing skill of Eric Swanson, this book would not exist.

A special thank-you to Carole DeSanti and Emma Sweeney, who both carried the torch for this project.

And finally, great appreciation for my publisher, Joel Fotinos; my editor, Sara Carder; and everyone at TarcherPerigee who made this book a reality.

If you enjoyed this book, visit

www.tarcherperigee.com

and sign up for TarcherPerigee's e-newsletter to receive special offers, updates on hot new releases, and articles containing the information you need to live the life you want.

tarcherperigee

LEARN. CREATE. GROW.

Connect with the TarcherPerigee Community

. . .

Stay in touch with favorite authors

Enter giveaway promotions

Read exclusive excerpts

Voice your opinions

Follow us

TarcherPerigee

@TarcherPerigee

@TarcherPerigee

If you would like to place a bulk order of this book, call 1-800-733-3000.